CITY SPECULATIONS

CITY SPECULATIONS

EDITED BY PATRICIA C. PHILLIPS

QUEENS MUSEUM OF ART
PRINCETON ARCHITECTURAL PRESS

PUBLISHED BY

Queens Museum of Art

New York City Building

Flushing Meadows Corona Park

Queens, New York 11368

AND

Princeton Architectural Press

37 East 7th Street

New York, NY 10003

ISBN 1-56898-077-9

Library of Congress Cataloging-in-Publication Data
for this title is available from the publisher.

EDITED BY

Mark Lamster

DESIGNED BY

Sara E. Stemen

Printed and bound in the United States

For a free catalog of other titles from Princeton Architectural Press,
call toll free: 1.800.722.6657 or visit http://www.papress.com.

CONTENTS

PREFACE

CARMA C. FAUNTLEROY

CENTRALLY located within the Queens Museum of Art, *The Panorama of the City of New York* occupies close to one-third of the museum's exhibition space. Its sheer immensity awed visitors to the 1964–65 World's Fair, for which it was created, and visitors continue to be overwhelmed by it today. Founded in 1972, the museum is housed in the fair's New York City Building, now operated by the City Department of Parks and Recreation. As a condition of occupancy, the museum is responsible for the ongoing presentation of the *Panorama* to the public. Projects like *City Speculations* are the means for bringing the model to life and imbuing it with the sense of urban dynamism that defines New York City.

Until recently, visitors could view the *Panorama* only from the north and west. Seen from a darkened mezzanine, the *Panorama* was obscured by a glass partition. From 1988 through 1989, however, the *Panorama* gallery was remodeled by architect Rafael Viñoly. Now, a glass-paneled railing encloses a walkway that ascends along the entire perimeter of the model, permitting a more direct visual experience from all sides. Accompanying the renovation of the gallery was a massive refurbishment of the *Panorama* itself. Today, it is easier than it has ever been to find one's own home and place of work on the surface of the model.

The museum's permanent exhibition, *A Panoramic View: The History of the New York City Building and Its Site,* provides the original context for and history of the fabrication of the *Panorama*. *City Speculations* carries this historical view into the present and beyond. Incorporating the media and methodologies of contemporary urban planning, *City Speculations* defines the city as a vibrant composition of disparate visions. In so doing, it restores the relevance of the *Panorama* to the museum's audience.

City Speculations was both conceived and organized by guest curator Patricia C. Phillips, Associate Professor and Chair of the Art Department at the State University of New York, New Paltz. Her intelligence and commitment have made it a success. Advisors Dennis Ferris, Frances Halsband, and Mildred Schmertz provided invaluable expertise. We are also grateful for the advice of Rosalie Genevero, Sharon Haar, Richard Plunz, William Rhoads, Anne Rieselbach, Laura Rosen, Bernard Tschumi, and Karen van Lengen. The research assistance of Guy Szeto and Adam Weinstein, and the installation work of Geoffrey Detrani and Jason Detrani also contributed to the success of the project. We also offer special thanks to Dorothy Howitt of the Art Department at SUNY, New Paltz. Of course, the realization of *City Speculations* would not have been possible without the tremendous enthusiasm of all of the exhibitors, who generously shared their ideas, energy, and vision. We especially wish to extend our gratitude to Kevin Lippert and the staff of Princeton Architectural Press for their professional assistance in the production of this volume.

As executive director of the museum, I wish to thank the Board of Trustees for their support of this project, as well as the entire museum staff, who brought it to fruition. In addition to the noteworthy guidance of Jane Farver, Director of Exhibitions, and Sharon Vatsky, Curator of Education, we appreciate the efforts of: Christina Yang, Carol Potter, Arnold Kanarvogel, and Steven Jo in the Curatorial Department; Paula Sharp, Ruth Magnusson, and Lisa Calandriello in the Development Department; Robert Mahoney, Public Information Officer; Mary T. Brown, Comtroller; Facilities Manager Louis Acquavita and Chief of Security Anthony Kemper; Hasie Sirisena, Assistant to the Executive Director; and members of the museum's business, development, education, and security departments.

With the assistance of Queens Borough President Claire Shulman and the New York City Council, the Museum is supported in part by public funds from the New York City Department of Cultural Affairs. Additional funding is provided by the New York State Legislature and the New York State Council on the Arts.

INTRODUCTION: PORTRAYING THE CITY

PATRICIA C. PHILLIPS

Cities aren't villages; they aren't machines; they aren't works of art; and they aren't telecommunications stations. They are spaces for face to face contact of amazing variety and richness. They are spectacle—and what is wrong with that?[1]

T H E *Panorama of the City of New York*, commissioned by Robert Moses for the 1964–65 New York World's Fair, may be the great summary image of a modern fortified city. In spite of its bold proportions and ambitious scope, it projects a finite and self-contained representation of New York. Like a specimen segregated for study, it is removed from its regional and environmental context. It is a still, silent picture—albeit a magnificent and seductive one—of the contemporary city. In its brilliant verisimilitude there is a haunting absence of the

1 Elizabeth Wilson, *The Sphinx in the City: Urban Life, the Control of Disorder, and Women* (Berkeley: University of California Press, 1991), 158.

complexities and turmoil that animate urban life and comprise the character of New York—or any other city. Astonishingly broad, we skim the surface of the *Panorama*, but there are few places to pause and reflect.

In February 1960 Moses accepted his final major position as the World's Fair Corporation president. It was the last in a long tally of titles—many held concurrently—that Moses acquired in the course of his remarkable career in public service. During his lengthy, influential, and fractious tenure as New York City's ultimate "power broker," he was credited with the development of beaches, bridges, housing, parks, recreation areas, and roadways. Moses was responsible for an astounding array of public works, including Flushing Meadows Park, Grand Central Parkway, Jones Beach, Stuyvesant Town, and the Triborough Bridge, to name just a few. But he has also been, justifiably, demonized for his ruthless and autocratic methods, his undemocratic social policies, and a misguided vision of the future of cities.[2]

As the principal organizer of this extravaganza, Moses enjoyed the enviable position and unchallenged authority to represent the twentieth-century city that he had helped shape. With the megalomaniacal zeal that characterized all of his work, he engineered an exposition of magnificent proportions and titillating diversions at Flushing Meadows Park in Queens. But Moses' long-term motivation for orchestrating the ephemeral fair—and an objective he had set at the 1939 World's Fair—was to create a new major urban park in Flushing to rival Manhattan's Central Park. Both in the geographic and popular center of a growing, reconfigured city, the new park—which he planned to name for himself—would have culminated his controversial career in public life.

Favoring the formulaic over the innovative, Moses followed the template that he had used for the 1939 fair in planning its successor. Consequently, the later exposition attempted to reproduce but never rivaled the enthralling, "brave new world" qualities promoted twenty-five years earlier at the same site. Moses' grandiose preoccupations were conspicuously evi-

2 With its apocalyptic title and voluminous content, Robert Caro's Pulitzer Prize-winning biography, *The Power Broker: Robert Moses and the Fall of New York* (New York: Alfred A. Knopf, 1974), is most responsible for revealing Moses' role as New York's "master builder."

dent in a trio of cartographic attractions. The Unisphere, a 140 foot high steel construction of the Earth's globe designed by Gilmore Clark and built by the U.S. Steel Corporation, became the fair's logo and remains an enduring feature at the site.

In the New York State Pavilion, Governor Nelson Rockefeller, architect Philip Johnson, and the Texas Oil Corporation (Texaco) marshaled forces to create a spectacular floor mosaic representing the New York State road maps distributed at Texaco gas stations. Today, at the pavilion's haunting ruins, there remain faint traces of the map, now fractured by large cracks and thickly overgrown with grasses and weeds.

The *Panorama*, the third monumental and laborious representational endeavor, was enthusiastically guided by Moses. For the New York City Pavilion, the only remaining structure used for both the 1939 and 1964–65 fairs, Moses commissioned the architectural modeling firm Lester Associates to construct a 1 inch : 100 feet scale model of New York City. Including all five boroughs, the nearly 10,000 square foot model would provide exquisite detail, voluminous information, and privileged views of the city.

The model's epic dimensions accommodated an obsession for detail: the city's 771 miles of shoreline, every street, and over 830,000 buildings were included in the Moses-inspired model. It took three years and almost $675,000 to build. At its unveiling, it was heralded as the "World's Largest Scale Model." Thirty years later this remains a legitimate, if vacuous, claim. As Marc H. Miller has noted, "With its colossal scale and down-to-earth factual literalness, the *Panorama* clearly reflected the distinctive tastes of Robert Moses."[3] Today, it remains a poignant, if melancholic and nostalgic, symbol of his legacy.

Lester Associates' contract with the World's Fair Corporation allowed for only a one percent margin of error in the construction of the model, a puzzlingly impossible requirement given the dynamic nature of urbanism.[4] How can error and accuracy be measured when the city

3 Marc H. Miller, *The Panorama of New York City* (New York: Queens Museum of Art, 1990), 14.

4 Ibid., 19.

is, as Jean-Paul Sartre describes, a "moving landscape for its inhabitants?" Despite the impossibility of their task, the model-makers analyzed and assimilated data from a number of representational resources in order to make an "error free" depiction of the 320 square-mile city. This material included: tax and insurance maps, vertical and oblique aerial photographs, Sanborn Maps, contour maps produced by the U.S. Geological Survey, and thousands of photographs of individual structures. Mixing representational veracity with other graphic conventions to ensure legibility, selected buildings and spaces were color-coded to classify typologies and city services that Moses deemed significant.

Since its renovation and reopening in the fall of 1994, viewers have circled the model in relative quiet. But as visitors entered the New York City Pavilion when the fair first opened, the audio-taped voice of Robert Wagner, then mayor of New York City, directed them to a scale model of the city of New Amsterdam circa 1660. Lilliputian in comparison to its sequestered companion, visitors could then only encounter the *Panorama* via a tracked-car ride that circled the perimeter of the model, simulating views from 3,000 to 20,000 feet. Traveling through a day-to-night lighting cycle, fair-goers orbited the gigantic model as the amplified voice of Lowell Thomas recounted the story of "the greatest city on earth." The theatrical nature of the *Panorama*, if diminished in its second reincarnation, remains disarmingly seductive.

The single-minded spectacle of the *Panorama* was, in many ways, Moses' tribute to himself at a time when his career and credibility were subject to challenge and ridicule. Although his career spanned over four decades, his work after World War II generally reflects an insatiable desire for power and a decline of vision. Although he predicted that the model would serve as an exceptional planning tool for the future—an incomparable resource for a new generation of city planners—it was, in fact, used as such only sporadically after the conclusion of the fair, and was virtually ignored following Moses' retirement from public life in the 1970s. A dinosaur in terms of any practical application, this embodiment of Moses' urban vision inevitably confirmed its own irrelevance, if not obsolescence. It is, in fact, no small irony that he advocated this titanic "planning" resource as the conclusive statement of a career that often avoided, demeaned, and suppressed long-term urban planning.

This remarkable exercise in heroic cartography and self-hagiography has been reinvented, rejuvenated, and revised, and now occupies the central space of the Queens Museum of Art, the current occupant of the New York City Building. Returned to Lester Associates in the early 1990s, the model was updated to represent the contemporary city. Buildings and other structures were extracted and added, recording the debilitating erasures and frantic additions in different areas of the city. Almost all structural amendments and deletions that have occurred in the past three decades have made their mark on the "new" *Panorama*. Without being beneficiaries to "before and after" portraits, viewers can only imagine the breadth and depth of change. Instead, they encounter a freeze frame of the present just as fair-goers experienced a city frozen in time at the midpoint of one of history's most fractious decades. The sense of volatile, sometimes violent, urban transformation is not codified in this model.

In spite of its amended, "contemporary" presentation, the *Panorama* is a paradoxical image; an obsessive and anachronistic form of urban representation. Now placed in the center of an art museum, visitors enter a small, discrete doorway to ascend a pedestrian ramp that encircles the model. At several points around the circumference, the programmed route leads onto glass balconies that extend out over the model, offering views other than the strictly peripheral. Less inhibited than most adult visitors, children from the many school groups that visit the *Panorama* often lie face down on the glass outcroppings to affect their own aerial views of the city.

Still, the *Panorama* depicts, as Moses ordained that it would, seamless, distant, and supposedly timeless views of the city's density and accretive sprawl. It is concurrently a plan, map, model, and portrait. In its reconstituted status as a collectible artifact or "art object," it is of significant historical if questionable aesthetic interest. It remains an uncritical representation of the—dubious—efficacy of the master plan, the unifying view, and the totalizing narrative. Compelling but never comprehensive, the *Panorama* manifests the ideological coding inherent in all forms of urban representation. With all that is visualized, viewers confront what they overlook about the city; for all that is evident, they are affected by what is absent.

The model's titanic dimensions and static presentation both clarify and complicate ideas about the temporal and mutable dimensions of cities and communities. How are these dynamic dimensions depicted? Are there representational strategies or technologies that feature and privilege change over stasis? With the intention of investigating exploratory and analytical work that "re-presents" the contemporary and future city, *City Speculations* seeks a response to the *Panorama*. Particular consideration has been given to creative propositions that engage particular sites and specific issues; projects whose strategies and forms have the capacity to proliferate in other areas of the city. Microscopic in comparison to the sweeping scope of the *Panorama*, in the work assembled here readers might discover an intimacy and immediacy in urbanism that the *Panorama* suppresses. Whereas the great model is a deductive exercise inviting conclusions about parts based on the whole, the forms of analysis, interpretation, and representation that comprise this volume are inductive. They are visions that offer productive, instrumental glimpses of aspects of the city, and they seek a collective comprehension.

Speculation engenders ideas about thinking and seeing, knowledge and vision. All forms of representation are inherently biased and support particular views of the city. Who is doing the representing? What is being presented? These are questions that remain in the foreground of contemporary cultural discourse. *City Speculations* presents and explores the different visions, means, methodologies, and intentions of urban representation. Using both the New York City metropolitan region and the *Panorama* as site and subject, these projects include a range of representational strategies and lenses through which the late-twentieth-century city can be visualized. Four projects directly respond to the *Panorama*—those of Mojdeh Baratloo and Clifton Balch, Newark Metametrics, Kyong Park with William Cathcart, and Wellington Reiter. An unanticipated fifth, by Richard Plunz with Victoria Benatar, Maria Gomez, Hubert Klumpner, and Erich Proedl, emerged from the *Panorama*'s renovation. The ten remaining projects present computer animations, drawings, environmental simulations, maps, videos, works in progress, and other forms of documentation. Together, they provoke the *Panorama* into a spirited conversation about urban representation.

Regardless of whether the contributors question or contest the Moses model, all of the work either intentionally or implicitly responds to the Queens Museum's centerpiece. The diversity of views presented makes clear that no single representation of the city is objective, comprehensive, benign, or true, and that all depictions of the city are informed by and inscribe a particular point of view. The museum invited contributors to begin new explorations, to develop ongoing projects, to take inquiries in new directions, or to usher ideas in germination to new levels of realization. *City Speculations* was, from the outset, framed as a research opportunity rather than a conclusive display of finished work. As such, these projects invite questions. What do different models, maps, and images of the city enable people to examine or force them to overlook? How do the diverse forms of urban representation affect the way we understand New York? How have the profound changes in imaging technologies influenced perception, planning, and design? The projects that comprise *City Speculations* are situated both metaphorically and, in the context of their position on the museum's floor, physically at points of mediation between the actual city and its ultimate representation.

There are connections and metaphors that animate these collective investigations. Postmodern theory has challenged notions of a unified self and a universal subject. This has allowed us to understand that contemporary issues of urban representation align with questions of identity. And if identity is understood as a negotiable, mutable, and nomadic subject, cities must also be explored and represented as transitional, layered, and often contradictory environments. Yet, with the *Panorama*, there remains a unifying, dogmatic coherence; a singular, infallible aspect to the views that it offers. The objective of *City Speculations* is, however, not to deride the Moses concept of urbanism, but to show its intentional objectives and latent limitations.

For all of his commitment to parkways and the vast arterial systems of New York, Moses paradoxically required a fixed image of the city. And it is just this fixity that the architects, artists, and designers included in *City Speculations* destabilize. Nomadism is an apt metaphor for the urban condition, for as individuals apprehend and understand the city through their own repetitious and fortuitous patterns of movement, they encounter an urban context that is circulatory and shifting. People experience and visualize the city as a transitive and temporal site. These projects contest any fixed, dominant scopic regime, and celebrate the faceted textures of spectacle.

In contrast to the epic narrative of the *Panorama*, *City Speculations* can be understood as an anthology of short stories written by many authors, representing a diversity of viewpoints. It is an anthology that establishes the connective tissue between the *Panorama*, the quintessential simulacrum of a city, and the city itself, the reality of the many iconographies that constitute urbanity.

Anthologies are never authoritative. Optimistically, they are collections of evidence that signal an atmospheric reality, an ether that surrounds and permeates perception. But it is in the concurrence and confederation of collected visions that readers of the city discover the freedom and possibility to honor many different stories, to let cities be both the symbols and repositories of cultural values. The objective of *City Speculations* is to introduce a spirited dialog in contrast to the strident monolog of the *Panorama*.

It is interesting to note that many of the contributors to *City Speculations* teach at colleges and universities. As educators, they are constructing the pedagogical structures for the next generation of architects, designers, and planners. Together, they ask questions about cause and effect, observation and meaning. While avoiding didacticism, there is an unmistakable instructional potential in this collection of projects. There are lessons formulated, inquiries pursued, and assumptions aired. The contributors to *City Speculations*, if not actively shaping the city, are undoubtedly influencing what it will become. They inscribe the theories that infiltrate practice. If the *Panorama* never fulfilled Moses' purported objectives as a powerful planning tool, *City Speculations* nonetheless confirms that it is a provocative teaching resource. Ironically, by challenging its effectiveness and relevance as urban representation, the contributors confirm its resonance as an educational instrument.

One month after Moses accepted the position of World's Fair Corporation president, the artist Jean Tinguely installed his own *Homage to New York* in the sculpture garden of the Museum of Modern Art. He found the components for the project in the dumps of New Jersey and the shops of Canal Street. Using his own panoply of devices, including bicycle wheels, old motors, piano parts, a go-cart, batteries, tubes, and a firearm, Tinguely's experimental, idiosyncratic sculpture was set into motion in order to self-destruct. At its opening—and closing—on 17 March 1960, it gyrated in spectacular fashion, yet failed to successfully complete its kamikaze mission. A tepid fire erupted and the New York City Fire Department reluctantly extinguished it. In the end, the remaining charred pieces of the installation were discarded—returned to the landfills that the artist frequented. As Billy Kulver observed, "All the rest was memory and pictures."[5]

At virtually the same moment that Tinguely sought fire and chaos to represent the city, Moses set out

5 Pontus Hulten, *Jean Tinguely: A Magic Stronger than Death* (New York: Abbeville Press, 1987), 77.

to freeze and preserve it. For all of his notable work, Moses never understood that the movement and velocity of parkways could be metaphors for the contemporary city, a concept promoted by many contemporary architects, planners, and theorists. He sought ways to circumvent and transgress the city, never envisioning that circulation might have some connection its systemic structures. Moses kept scrutinizing the silent, still picture long after it was out of focus. In contrast, Tinguely sought an image, a gesture, and a spectacular and ephemeral moment as the most appropriate analog of the city. In vividly different ways, both the *Panorama* and *Homage* have left their memorable imprints on their host museums as well as the city beyond. *City Speculations* seeks meaning in the points between fixity and temporality, between the inevitable and the imagined city.

THE NEW YORK PANORAMA:
A PARADOXICAL VIEW

M. CHRISTINE BOYER

I**T** seems paradoxical that Robert Moses would choose, at the end of his career, to display a comprehensive view of his master works. Moses, who controlled the landscape of New York for nearly fifty years, neither believed in the process of planning nor ever produced a master plan for the many projects he built. Why did he employ the totalized view encompassed by a panorama—a scale model of miniaturized buildings, streets, parks, and bridges—to reveal his command over the physical reality of the city and to display the marvelous record of his reign? Why not rely on the most advanced techniques of simulation that the 1960s could offer in order to entertain and visually stimulate the spectator? He could have used photographic projections to achieve the effect of greater illusion, or he might have explored the sight and sound simulations of Cinerama, a popular medium of projected three-dimensional images. There is always a pressure in popular entertainment to move from mere representation to the higher technical arts of simulation, where the experience of reality and illusion are confounded in the production of more fantastical worlds. Why, then, did Robert Moses revert to displaying the works of his masterful hand in the nostalgic replication of a nineteenth-century medium, the panorama, at the 1964–65 New York World's Fair?

There are many reasons why Moses may have selected the more archaic techniques of representation embodied in a scale model over the more theatrical effects produced by more sophisticated forms of simulation. One can assume that he wanted to emphasize the physical experience of looking in order to accentuate the sense of amazement and surprise produced by the marvelous view of his efforts. The assumption can likewise be made that he hoped that spectators would be astonished when confronted with a building program that they knew of from newspaper accounts but had never envisioned in entirety, and that this astonishment would implicate spectators in the aura of wonderment created by the *Panorama*. Perhaps he also knew that the historical acceptance of his work depended on visitors substituting the *Panorama*'s landscape view of his completed project for the experience of confusion and disruption that industrial change and modernization had entailed. It can be argued as well that Moses wished to demonstrate his control over the city, to underscore that he was the master draftsman, the rational technician who held the power to transform this view. More spectacular means of representation—like Cinerama—might only have diverted attention from his accomplishments by accentuating the technical apparatus used to create the illusion.[1] Finally, Moses may also have desired a public demonstration of his accomplishment, a social event and record for the collective memory of the city. Such an event would necessarily require a shared visual experience. Consequently, he would have wanted to avoid isolating the spectator in the darkness necessary for projected images or filmed events.

Yet even panoramas display a bias for showing everything without divulging anything. Like a successful magic show, they depend on their techniques being invisi-

1. The following account draws a distinction between representation and simulation and follows closely the argument that Don Slater developed in "Photography and Modern Vision: the Spectacle of 'Natural Magic,'" in Chris Jenks, ed. *Visual Culture* (New York: Routledge, 1995), 218–237.

ble. While panoramas may transform the material world into a new reality, they reveal only their power to transform, never demonstrating how this process takes place. In 1787, the inventor of panoramas, Robert Barker, claimed that they presented *"nature á coup d'oeil"*—a silent still life with the power to capture appearances and command the wonders of nature. The spectators of one of Barker's panoramas, after traveling through a darkened tunnel, climbed a staircase and were suddenly deposited on a platform fixed at the center of a centrifugal view. Although they could never approach the horizon of this perspectival model, viewers were nevertheless immersed in a virtual space that might be mistaken for the real, or at least taken for a good facsimile of it.

The early success of the panorama relied on the artistic power of both scene-painters, whose seamless dissolves could simulate the passing of time, and the wizardry of technicians, who could produce the illusion of movement by projecting light across a model. These feats of artifice and mechanical invention were sufficient to create the illusion that reality had been inexplicably transformed by secret or invisible technique. Not only did panoramas faithfully represent the detail, texture, and look of actual objects and events, but they served as "mirror[s] with a memory," reproducing events and objects from the past and projecting them into the present.[2] Disbelief could be playfully suspended, for the spectator knew, as part of the theatrical experience, that it was actually the technique of the scene-painter, the mechanisms of projection, and the realistic props and objects that had produced the effect of the real.[3] Such effects may well have been important for Moses, as he clearly intended to have his panorama call attention to his power over the topography of the city.

Between 1860 and 1910, panoramas reached their height of popularity, not only achieving the realistic representation of space, but providing a sensation of motion as well. They served as a kind of pre-cinematic, animated newspaper that called on spectators to make connections between the view

2. This is how Oliver Wendell Holmes described the daguerreotype in 1859. Quoted in Slater, ibid., 218.

3. Ibid.

represented and contemporary events reported by the press.[4] Thus, Charles Castellani's panorama entitled "Le Tout Paris" triumphed by grouping the figures of various celebrities around the well known Place de l'Opéra. One reviewer exclaimed, "no better place could have been chosen in this shining and noisy Paris to represent Parisian life in all its ardor, vigor, and feverishness."[5] It appears that this simple, circular panorama—a painting that did not compete with other panoramas of the day in terms of verisimilitude—was nevertheless a grand success because its subject matter alone was sufficient to animate its view. It provided a lifelike rendition of a moment taken from popular discourse that had already been narrated in the press.[6]

During the late nineteenth century, Paris displayed a kind of "panoramania." When the famous Musée Grévin wax museum opened in 1882, it became an immediate success, attracting half a million visitors annually. Modeled in part on Madame Tussaud's London wax museum, it was founded by journalist Arthur Meyer and newspaper caricaturist Alfred Grévin. They intended this museum to mimic the newspaper, offering a random juxtaposition of tableaux similar to the manner in which newspaper columns presented readers with series of unconnected stories. They changed these tableaux often, promising that their displays would "represent the principal current events with scrupulous fidelity and striking precision. . . . [It is to be] a living museum."[7] In order to heighten the effect of realism, installations were furnished with authentic accessories: a model of Victor Hugo held the author's real pen; the effigy of Marat was displayed in the revolutionary's actual tub.[8] Thus, the museum offered the spectator the novelty of visualizing familiar events, people, and stories in exacting detail at a time when photographs were not easily reproduced and had yet to accompany newspaper reports. Furthermore, these views required that spectators willingly acknowledge the link between known facts or public events and their representations.

4. Vanessa R. Schwartz, "Cinematic Spectatorship before the Apparatus," in Linda Williams ed. *Viewing Positions: Ways of Seeing Film* (New Brunswick: Rutgers University Press, 1994), 107.
5. Ibid., 97–98.
6. Ibid., 105–111.
7. Quoted by Schwartz, ibid., 94.
8. Ibid., 95.

These simulations also enabled visitors to inhabit multiple perspectives and to experience the surprise of seeing things that one might not ordinarily see. For example, in 1889 the museum presented a tableau of the Eiffel Tower before it had been officially opened—a chance for the public to glimpse the magnificent views the tower would soon offer. Three sights were cleverly combined into one privileged view. Spectators saw Gustav Eiffel and several exposition officials inspecting the tower in mid-construction; workers who had stopped to watch those very dignitaries; and a panoramic view of Paris from the second level of the tower. Surely this would have pleased Robert Moses, for he too wanted to ensure that spectators made connections between projects well known from daily experience or newspaper reports and the surprising totalized vision that his panorama displayed.

Using the most advanced technical means, three-dimensional tableaux vivants, along with panoramas, dioramas, magic-lantern shows, photographs, and stereoscopic views offered the nineteenth-century spectator new kinds of visual realism. These new kinds of realism, however, may have had characteristics that Robert Moses would have wanted to avoid. Not only did these simulations assume the viewpoint of a journalist or an artist, but they required a technical apparatus in order to organize, manage, and produce their three-dimensional effects. Consequently, it was not just representational realism but mechanical or instrumental wizardry that enthralled audiences in the late nineteenth century. They flocked to theatrical spectacles and thrilled at scenographic displays magically transformed by mechanical devices. By attending these types of shows, Victorian society gradually learned to live with modern machines and mechanical processes. Technical accomplishments became spectacles in themselves, for at that time "to represent, to know, to transform [became] not only mutually reinforcing but united activities, three forms of appropriation of the material world which both produce[d] and assimilate[d] the modern experience of command and control."[9]

Modern realism enabled the world to be   **9.** Slater, Op. cit., 222.

described in "factual form," supposedly uncompromised by theory, values, or magical events. It enabled sight itself to be produced by the same industrial techniques that created the objects of sight, thereby calling attention to the technical apparatus of vision. Paradoxically, once the world had been deprived of wonder through its instruments of realistic vision, once occult and supernatural effects had been destroyed through so much understanding, the nineteenth century attempted to re-enchant its visual field in theatrical events, visual spectacles, and quasi-magical shows. By hiding the apparatus of display and highlighting the artifice of re-creation, it relied on the magic of inexplicable processes and special effects. Hence, no matter how great the factual details of realism were, there was always a pressure to move from mere representation and factual understanding to simulation and the demonstration—not explication—of how effective illusions and wonders were produced. In contrast to this rational and instrumental control over material reality lay a willingness to suspend disbelief and become pleasurably immersed in fantastical worlds.[10]

Although dioramas, panoramas, and even wax museums had been popular forms of entertainment in the late eighteenth century, they nevertheless experienced a revival of interest at the end of the nineteenth century. As witnessed in the popular displays that the Musée Grévin presented, that era experienced an unquenchable desire for spectacle. As audiences grew more and more accustomed to seeing their world produced in realistic exactitude—demonstrating that one could appropriate, master, map, project, and reconstruct it—additional pleasure arose from the ability to simulate that world, from the special effects themselves. Wonder, once the result of excellence in draughtsmanship or a particular scenographer's theatrical skill was now dependent on the ability of mechanical techniques to produce an illusory space in which the spectator lost the sense of being in a constructed world. Thus, to take an example, the stereoscope—first displayed to the world at the Great Exhibition of 1851—created the illusion of three-dimensional

10. Ibid., 218–237.

depth, "enabling" the viewer to move into the surface of an image, look around its objects, and feel their solidity. As did many of the other nineteenth-century forms of spectacular illusion, the stereoscope cheated the senses by removing the marks of its own production.[11] Surely Moses would have wanted to avoid the mystical aura of such forms of artifice, for they might re-enchant the spectator's view and distract them from their awareness of his role as "master builder" and obscure the marks of his construction. Indeed, many of Moses' projects, in particular his bridges, were made out of brass in order to stand out in the mass of structures in the *Panorama*. Indeed, this older representational medium permitted viewers to make the linkages between events that they already knew of from years of newspaper reporting with the actual locations of those events within the *Panorama*'s landscape of the city. Now, they could verify and acknowledge just how comprehensive Moses' transformations had been.

The desire for greater realism always seems to push toward the simulation of three-dimensional images. Nothing illustrates this better than the development of Cinerama, an apparatus that projected multiple wide-angle images onto a spherically adapted screen. The evolution of this system began in 1937, when architect Ralph Walker approached film producer and special effects expert Fred Waller with the idea of creating a projected three-dimensional presentation for the 1939 World's Fair.[12] By the end of 1938, Laurance Rockefeller had joined Walker and Waller in the formation of the Vitarama Corporation, with the express goal of perfecting the machinery for projecting three-dimensional images. Waller, formerly the head of Paramount's special effects department and the technical mastermind of the new company, was already well aware that the exploitation of peripheral vision produced a sense of realism by stimulating the perception of three-dimensional depth. To compliment projected images, Waller experimented with sound systems that would augment a spectator's sensation of realism.

11. Ibid., 218–237.
12. The development of Cinerama is recounted in a 1950 letter by Fred Waller published as, "The Archeology of Cinerama," *Film History* 5 (1993): 289–297.

Waller, through Vitarama, produced three installations for the 1939 fair. The first, on the interior of the exhibition's Perisphere, was a projection of ten columns of figures marching in synchronicity to the fair's theme song. Another, developed for Kodak and known as the "Hall of Color," offered a panoramic projection of the company's Kodachrome slides on eleven different screens arranged in spherical sections. This slick presentation became the best attended commercial installation at the fair. Vitarama's third exhibit was a simulation of space travel developed for the American Museum of Natural History. Entitled "Time and Space," it consisted of a combination of moving and still images projected onto a curved surface. Together, these three exhibits captured the imaginations of American audiences, who had a seemingly insatiable appetite for ever more advanced modes of representation.

Never afraid to follow a promising trend, corporate America sought to capitalize on the powerful impact of Vitarama's new methods of projection. Following World War II, Time, Inc. called on Waller to develop a promotional presentation for *Life* magazine glorifying the postwar American way of life. The result, "The New America," was so successful that the State Department, recognizing its value as a propaganda tool, appropriated the show and presented it to German and Japanese audiences who gave it rave reviews.

Banking on a record of popular success, the 1946 formation of the Cinerama Corporation allowed Waller time and money to develop a sight and sound apparatus for commercial entertainment. His subsequent experiments revealed that a cylindrical screen minimized the distortions of side views created by projection onto a spherical screen. With Cinerama, Waller sought to take advantage of the way the mind comprehends space, such as the gradual graying or bluing of objects as they move away from the eye, or the unconscious awareness that objects directly in front of the eye are plainly enlarged and objects on the periphery of vision move rapidly by. Waller experimented with Cinerama's sound system as well: six different audio channels seemed to be optimal, allowing a uniform volume of sound to travel across the screen and beyond its limits, all the while enhancing the depth of that sound as it moved away from and toward the audience. Cinerama's elaborate machinery served to trick the senses and immerse the viewer in a completely simulated space. It focused the spectator's wonder on the technical apparatus that produced the show and not on its actual content or creator.

No doubt, all of these modern arts of simulation were known by and available to Robert Moses, but he willfully chose to avoid them. Was it because they were ideal techniques for re-enchanting a realistic view with the magic of unknown processes? World's fairs were often the proving grounds for those combining technological innovation with ideological discourse in order to enable spectators to envision worlds yet to be actualized. Robert Moses, however, wanted to present a record of his actual achievements, to represent the last fifty years of his construction as a completed tableau. He thus appropriately selected the more archaic theatrical event of a panorama in model form.

QUEENS CONJECTURE

MOJDEH BARATLOO AND CLIFTON BALCH

The Total Built Volume of New York City

The Area of Central Park

Manhattan Street Grid (overlaid on P)

$$C < (P - G) \times T$$

The Height of the World Trade Center Towers

The Area of the Center Towers

Above: $C < (P-G) \times T$. Photo: Paul Warchol.

Opposite: stills from the computer animated fly-through of $C < (P-G) \times T$.

Computer animation created with Mark Watkins.

T**HE** *Panorama of the City of New York* strives towards a literal projection of the city. It displays New York's physicality—its breadth and its magnitude—as a precise model of reality. Yet the view is a disturbingly unfamiliar image of the city dissipating over vast space. As one circles the *Panorama* via Rafael Viñoly's ever ascending ramp, there is a metaphorical removal from the experiential realities of the city as we know it.

$C<(P-G)xT$ is a counter-model created as an alternative to the *Panorama*. Built to scale, like the *Panorama*, the "factual" information presented in this abstraction simultaneously illuminates both the objective and subjective qualities of the city.

As a physical model $C<(P-G)xT$ represents the equivalent of the total volume of all of the buildings in the five boroughs of New York City. This abstract calculation is made physically intelligible through its reference to three iconic infrastructural elements of the city: the park, the tower, and the grid. The dimensions of the counter-model are scaled to the length and width of Central Park and the height of the World Trade Center

towers. Inside of this envelope, randomly-composed, block-like elements are set within the grid of fifty-one streets and three avenues that Central Park overlays, creating a dense interlocking configuration. A computer animated fly-through of $C<(P-G)xT$ illuminates the interi-

or of this new urban analogue. In distinction to the peripheral experience of the *Panorama*, this video provides access to the dense interior of the counter-model.

As an abstract representation, $C<(P-G)xT$ acts as a contrast to the literalness of the *Panorama*. It is an analogical model of urban form that attempts to conjure the multiple experiential realities of New York City—its compression, vitality, spontaneity, danger, flow, chaos, and wonder.

Above and opposite: stills from the computer animated fly-through of $C < (P-G) x$

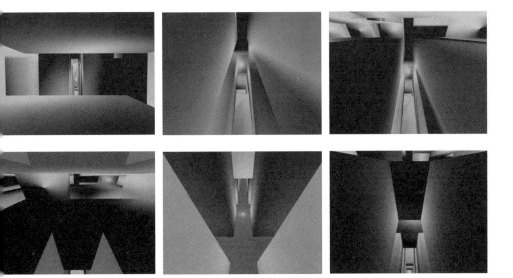

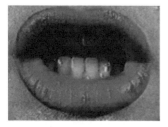

Hey you, wanna buy a pair of tickets behind home plate?

Hey you, wanna buy something for nothing?

Hey you, wanna buy a vacant lot in midtown?

Hey you, wanna buy a second chance?

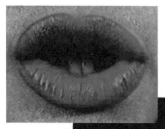

Hey you, wanna buy an authentic original, only one of its kind?

Hey you, wanna buy some motherly love?

Hey you, wanna buy an Ivy League education?

SOFT SELL

DILLER + SCOFIDIO

Hey you, wanna buy a ticket to paradise?

Hey you, wanna buy your name in lights?

Hey you, wanna buy a new suit that makes you look important?

Hey you, wanna buy a rare opportunity?

Hey you, wanna buy a left kidney?

Hey you, wanna buy a judge?

Hey you, wanna buy a turbo-charged, souped-up, shiny muscle car?

Hey you, wanna buy a vowel?

Hey you, wanna buy a place in heaven?

Hey you, wanna buy a one-year subscription?

Hey you, wanna buy an all-you-can-eat diet plan?

Hey you, wanna buy yourself some more time?

Hey you, wanna buy a brand new baby boy?

Hey you, wanna buy a new identity?

Hey you, wanna buy an unobstructed view of the skyline?

'I'm here for only one thing. The money.'[1] 'an ugly cow that gives a lot of milk.'[2] 'We bring a lot of tourists to this area. If not for us, this town would be dead

FORTY-SECOND STREET has always been defined by reversible values, an "unsightly" tourist site where the friction between decadence and delight produces a meeting ground of conflicting patronage. As the lyrics of the theme song of the musical *Forty-Second Street* state, it is a place where "the underworld can meet the elite." In this marketplace, successive forms of currency have continually supplanted one another. High society entertainment gave way to cabaret society at the turn of the century, which gave way

to the movie industry in the late 1920s, which gave way to popular amusements in the 1950s, which gave way to the overt marketing of flesh and drugs in the 1960s, which will give way to the interests of real estate and fashionable merchandising in the 1990s. With each change, the desire-producing apparatus adapts to accommodate and maintain the currency of the moment. The sustenance of the "object of desire," however, is dependent on the object's indefinite deferral.

Created in the summer of 1994, *Soft Sell* was originally located on Forty-second Street in the entrance of the former Rialto Theater, now an abandoned pornographic theater. Revised for *City Speculations*, it is now comprised of a small video screen on which a pair of sensuous, brilliant red lips make a series of solicitations. Set just below eye level in the wall, the lips are "naturally" proportioned and positioned. Beneath this screen, a horizontal line of quotations that refer to the Times Square area stretches across the exhibition space, culminating in a pair of Rolodexes that contain the addresses of the businesses and occupants of Forty-second Street.

1 Character from the film, *Forty-second Street*, 1932
2 Real estate broker
3 Male prostitute
4 Travis, from the film, *Taxi Driver*, 1976
5 *Time* magazine
6 *New Yorker* staff writer
7 Michael Eisner
8 Robert A.M. Stern

the animals come out at night: whores, skunk-pussies, buggers, queens, fairies, dopers, junkies. Sick. Venal. Some time, a REAL rain will come and wash ALL the

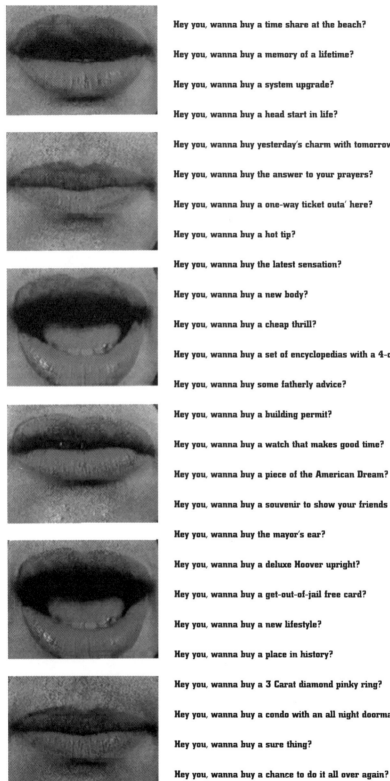

Hey you, wanna buy a time share at the beach?

Hey you, wanna buy a memory of a lifetime?

Hey you, wanna buy a system upgrade?

Hey you, wanna buy a head start in life?

Hey you, wanna buy yesterday's charm with tomorrow's comfort?

Hey you, wanna buy the answer to your prayers?

Hey you, wanna buy a one-way ticket outa' here?

Hey you, wanna buy a hot tip?

Hey you, wanna buy the latest sensation?

Hey you, wanna buy a new body?

Hey you, wanna buy a cheap thrill?

Hey you, wanna buy a set of encyclopedias with a 4-colour atlas?

Hey you, wanna buy some fatherly advice?

Hey you, wanna buy a building permit?

Hey you, wanna buy a watch that makes good time?

Hey you, wanna buy a piece of the American Dream?

Hey you, wanna buy a souvenir to show your friends and family?

Hey you, wanna buy the mayor's ear?

Hey you, wanna buy a deluxe Hoover upright?

Hey you, wanna buy a get-out-of-jail free card?

Hey you, wanna buy a new lifestyle?

Hey you, wanna buy a place in history?

Hey you, wanna buy a 3 Carat diamond pinky ring?

Hey you, wanna buy a condo with an all night doorman?

Hey you, wanna buy a sure thing?

Hey you, wanna buy a chance to do it all over again?

scum off the streets."4 "Such a splendid oxymoronic turn: a municipal code for discouraging tastefulness."5 "Let's get more counterfeit luxury goods out there."6 "Disney

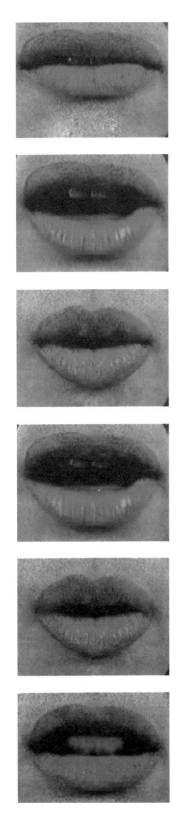

Hey you, wanna buy a piece of the action?

Hey you, wanna buy a place at the head of the line?

Hey you, wanna buy a winning combination?

Hey you, wanna buy a membership to the Club?

Hey you, wanna buy your place in the sun?

Hey you, wanna buy out the competition?

Hey you, wanna buy forgiveness for your sins?

Hey you, wanna buy a good night's sleep?

Hey you, wanna buy your 15 minutes in the spotlight?

Hey you, wanna buy a pair of gym shoes with air cushioned insoles?

Hey you, wanna buy a hundred shares of no-risk, blue chip stock?

Hey you, wanna buy a spin on the wheel of love?

Hey you, wanna buy a developer's dream package?

Hey you, wanna buy a new reputation?

Hey you, wanna buy some votes?

Hey you, wanna buy the fountain of youth?

Hey you, wanna buy a second opinion?

Hey you, wanna buy your way in?

Hey you, wanna buy someone to take the fall?

Hey you, wanna buy some peace of mind?

Hey you, wanna buy a piece of the rock?

Hey you, wanna buy tomorrow's memories today?

Hey you, wanna buy some quality dental work?

Hey you, wanna buy someone's death?

Hey you, wanna buy your kids the good life?

Hey you, wanna buy a full service secretary?

ll bring a cleaner, safer, more friendly environment."[7] "We're after vulgar heterogeneity. The goal is not a 'themed' simulacrum of honky tonk diversity, but the real thing."[8]

SWITCH

KELLER EASTERLING

NETWORK architecture arranges multiples—multiple sites, buildings, programs, and even multiple networks—in economies of exchange. It makes adjustments: subtractions, reversals, cycles, summations, and rotations. The results of these adjustments are relational in nature, rather than formal, although the relationships they create have enormous spatial and material consequences. *Switch* speculates about a city in which network adjusters alter master plans. Specifically, it examines the tactical adjustment of an urban transportation hub.

Communication networks involve flexible patterns of exchange between heterogeneous components of differing scales. Transportation networks, on the other hand, are generally segregated. Their development has been driven by cycles of expansion, redundancy, and obsolescence. The development of the highway interchange in America, for example, was not the result of a desire to connect different networks of transportation, but was rather the confirmation of a single dominant transportation system.

The redundancies that often result from multiple transportation systems establish a prospective field for the network adjuster. At the hubs where these systems converge, there is a need for an architecture not of building form, but of protocols for intermodality and intelligent switching. Like a mathematical function between multiple variables, a differential architecture at these interstices activates a number of networks at once. *Switch* is a framework for translations and transitions between such operating environments.

Switch operates at an intersection of networks in the Penn Station/Caemmemer Yards area. This site is largely devoted to storage and transportation infrastructure, with underground freight conduits and highway on-ramps leading to tunnels and terminals. Ringing the rail yards is an abandoned elevated track that has been slated for removal. There are also several small-scale warehouses, and parking lots for cars and other

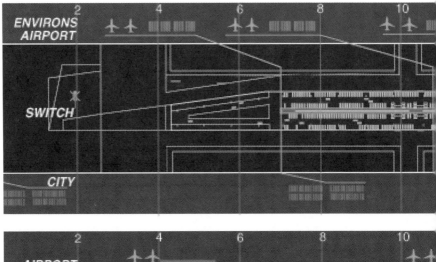

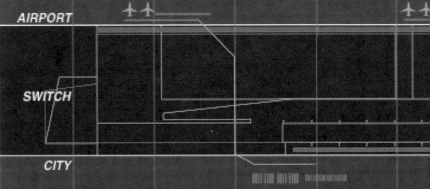

vehicles that access the Lincoln Tunnel, the Jacob K. Javits Convention Center, and Madison Square Garden. Lastly, there is the Lincoln Tunnel connection at Thirtieth Street, all that remains of Robert Moses' failed master plan for the Mid-Manhattan Elevated Expressway.

In the space vacated by the elevated track, *Switch* inserts transportation and storage programs joined to form a new kind of interface: an intermodal substation for freight, automobiles, and helicopters. A three thousand foot repeatable structure, extending from the tunnel entrance to the heliport, moves, sorts, and stores these vehicles, their cargo, and their passengers, according to

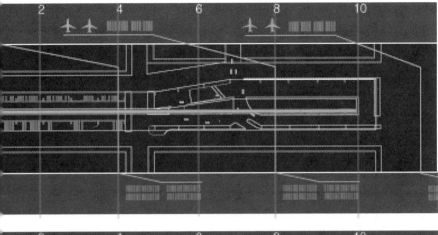

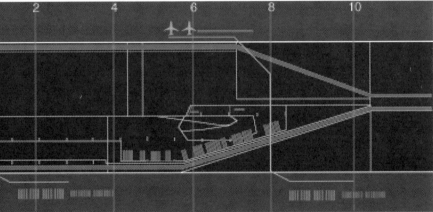

Time-lapse plans of the *Switch,* showing the upper and street levels (top) and the lower level (bottom). Freight and passengers are exchanged between levels and routed to their final destinations with maximum efficiency. Time is indicated along the top of the plans.

size and program. This hub mixes surface and air freight via an underground rail link to local airports and works interdependently with a new web of loading-dock sites embedded within its blocks. Trucks delivering to the hub quickly return to the road, leaving final delivery to smaller vehicles. An internal con-veyance system transports passengers within the structure.

The video that accompanies *Switch* employs a mixture of computer animation, real-time video, and still photography in order to create a cartoon-like sequence emphasizing rapid action and plastic mutability.

THE AMERICAN CONTEXT IN URBAN DESIGN

URBAN design in the United States is grounded in the Constitution's evolving definition of property and the rights and obligations attendant to the ownership and use of it. In an effort to balance the Enlightenment ideals of Lockean individualism and Rousseauistic communitarianism, the Constitution recognizes both the need to protect the public welfare and to protect private property from capricious governmental action. Indeed, the ownership and use of property in America remains a highly charged issue of almost mythic proportions, always open to public debate. This has led to the acceptance of extensive public participation in not only the formulation of the rules and regulations of urban design, but in the development of individual projects as well. It is in this context that Donald Appelyard, of the University of California, wrote:

The Environmental Simulation Center is directed by Michael Kwartler.

Opposite: Lower Manhattan 3D Geographic Information System, view from World Trade Center of prime space for residential conversion. Above: Photo realistic model of the Lincoln Center area showing existing conditions.

Planning decisions can, and frequently do, threaten the identity and status of certain groups, while enlarging the powers of others. . . . The environment is divided into "ours" and "theirs," the trees may be ours, the billboards theirs, the authentic ours, the phony theirs or ours. . . . The city and the natural environment are arenas of symbolic social conflicts and as such raise their own issues of social justice.[1]

Anglo-American empiricism and the legal system derived from it have tended to dominate urban planning and design decision making. The legal system's adversarial approach to adjudication is essentially a zero-sum game of winners and losers, and as most land-use lawyers will agree, it is not a good model for the planning and design of cities. While

[1] Donald Appelyard, "The Environment as a Social Symbol," *Journal of American Institute of Planners* 54, no. 143 (1979):152.

Above: Photo realistic model of the Lincoln Center area simulating zoning alternatives.

the adversarial approach does resolve disputes, it rarely creates a positive and constructive consensus for change, and it has not clearly defined the limits of the individual's rights and the public's interest in the use of property. Because these rights and interests are value laden and identity based, consensus building has emerged as a new paradigm for making physical planning decisions. This allows the broadest spectrum of individuals to relate to urban design proposals. In this context, we have come to understand that representations of urban form must communicate successfully to all of the participants in the debate, to the public at large.

SIMULATIONS AND THEIR USE

Traditionally, urban planning and design issues have been conveyed in words, numbers, and static images. Environmental simulation, by contrast, is dynamic and highly interactive. In addition to generating moving images, modeling and simulation techniques allow the viewer to step into the images and experience alternative proposals from an infinite variety of perspectives. In simulation, as in the real world, time and movement are in constant flux, making the viewer not

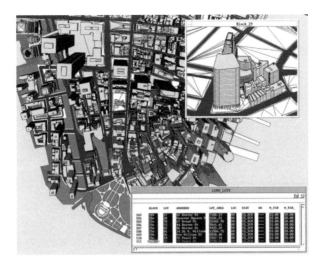

Top: Lower Manhattan 3D Geographic Information System. Proposal for historic distict. Above: Simulation of proposed Village Center for Princeton Junction, New Jersey created with the Environemental Simualtion Center's Kit-of-Parts.

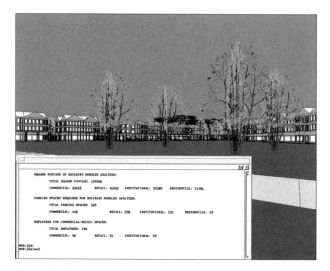

Above: Simulated eye-level view of the proposed Village Center for Princeton Junction accompanied by data derived from the Kit-of-Parts.

just an observer but an active participant. At the Center, two complementary techniques of simulation are employed: computer modeling and physical modeling. These can be used individually or in combination. Because it produces mathematically accurate images of data, computer modeling is principally applied to urban design issues that require quantitative analysis, such as zoning alternatives, micro-climate conditions, or growth management plans. Physical modeling, while not as mathematically precise as computer simulation, is photo-realistic and perceptually accurate, and can convincingly depict building textures, landscaping, and streetscape details. It is best suited to the depiction of specific sites, districts, and structures; for conveying how the environment will look and feel, particularly at the pedestrian level.

BEYOND THE ARRESTED IMAGE: REPRESENTATION IN URBAN DESIGN

The representation of cities has long been deeply connected to the history and politics of perception, and as such has been simultaneously liberating, constraining, and manipulative.

Typically, two-dimensional images picture the city as an idealized environment frozen in time. While liberating in one sense—the world is seen from an individual's singular point of view—static perspective drawings and photographs manipulate and control experience through the canonization of meaning in the images themselves. Their power, oddly, lies in defying both our experience and sense of the world as dynamic and filled with movement.

Digital technologies have the potential to provide richer representational environments that are responsive to what Kevin Lynch has described as the contingent and existential qualities of cities and parallel our own experience.

> Not only is the city an object which is perceived (and perhaps enjoyed) by millions of people of widely diverse class and character, but it is the product of many builders who are constantly modifying the structure for reasons of their own. While it may be stable in general outlines for some time, it is ever changing in details. Only partial control can be exercised over its growth and form. There is no final result, only a continuous secession of phases.[2]

Three-dimensional digital models, such as the one the Center has created for Lower Manhattan, include visual and non-visual information. This information is dynamically combined to allow viewers to perceive and interactively engage the model and the place it depicts. There is a latent egalitarian potential in these technologies that allows you to "have it your way."

If urban design is to become a more inclusive and egalitarian process, the representation of urban design must move beyond the idealized static image and embrace the messiness of the city. With its ability to image dynamic relationships and allow individuals to interactively take part in the design process, the computer will play a central role in this change.

2 Kevin Lynch, *Image of the City* (Cambridge: MIT Press, 1960), 2.

THE NOMAD MAPPING PROJECT

ANDREA KAHN

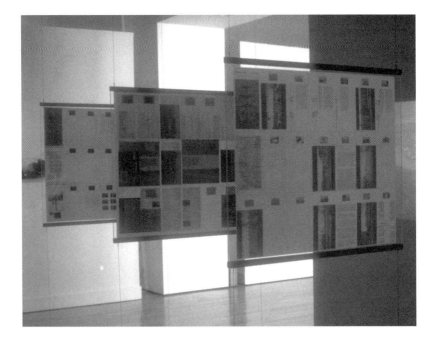

> Two important characteristics of maps should be noticed. A map is not the territory it represents, but, if correct, it has a similar structure to the territory, which accounts for its usefulness.
>
> ALFRED KORYBSKI,
> *SCIENCE AND SANITY*

I used to have a car. A red car filled with old, strange, dusty things randomly strewn around the back seat to keep thieves at bay. For the longest time an empty highball glass sat in the left rear ashtray, the mark of a stranger who had slept in my car one night in Ohio years before. In the glove compartment, I kept all of the road maps that I had ever bought; on the dashboard, I kept all of my red car toys, collected over thirteen years. After I moved to New York City, I would leave my sweltering apartment behind during hot summer nights, and take a drive in the car, opening all of the windows so that air could move around my body. When I got lost, I would go into the glove compartment with one hand to find my New York City map. This particular map was very old, and had been folded and unfolded so many times that it had split into pieces. Whenever I got lost, I could never seem to find the part of the map that corresponded to where I thought I was. Each time the remnants would surface and recombine in a new way, making whole new cities appear out of the bits and pieces of the old. When I sold my car, I kept the remains of that old map.

Why now go back? Why now introduce a new way of reading a book, instead of the one that moves, like life, from beginning to end, from birth to death? The answer is simple, because any new way of reading that goes against the matrix of time, which pulls us toward death, is a futile but honest effort to resist this inexorability of one's fate, in literature, if not in reality.... So, why then, must the reader always be like a police inspector, why must he always walk in his predecessor's every footstep? Why not let him at least zigzag somewhere?

MILORAD PAVIC, *LANDSCAPE PAINTED WITH TEA*

As an alternative to traditional plan depictions, the *Nomad Mapping Project* proposes a new way to represent the city. Since no city exists outside of the movement of time, and since all urban limits are impermanent, the complex spaces of the city will always be difficult to render with static models and two-dimensional views. The *Project* challenges the reductive propensity of conventional strategies of urban and architectural representation by exploring a productive web of intersections between urban artifacts, methods of observation, and modes of thought. The artifacts—photographs—record undervalued places in densely settled urban regions. The method of observation—from a moving point— brings new value to the otherwise overlooked condition of urban dynamism. The modes of thought—visual and verbal, critical and creative—propose an urban architecture predicated on multiple, simultaneous, and shifting experiences. Mirroring the city, these maps use diverse materials and voices to invent and reinvent the urban. To find one's way through them, the maps must be approached from many directions, many times over.

The *Nomad Mapping Project* is an open, urban work. A shifting point of reference, it is neither fixed nor stationary, but is fostered by a ubiquitous condition: the mobility of modern life, especially American life. It is a roving investigation, an account of trajectories drawn across transitional territory occasioned by movement and dedicated to architectural thought in motion. It is a game of chance, a project about looking: at things, at ideas, at language, at the very act of looking. The maps take to task the desire to arrive, and challenge the architect's tendency to become bound up with settlements: patterns on the landscape, contractual agreements, decisions towards definitive solutions. The *Project* is neither about buildings that move nor the temporary shelters erected by people on the move. Instead, it charts mobile ground, architecture as action. It traces the intersections of viewing bodies and a body of buildings often obscured from view. In part, this project is a plot. It reflects a mode of thought, a fabrication of observations rather

> A rosary is a map, a computer programme and Molloy's sixteen sucking stones are maps. A map is made so we can find our way from one place to another whether in nature or in the mind, not only once, but again and again.
>
> ANNE SEYMOUR, *RICHARD LONG*

than a conclusive construction. It refers to a mode of architectural observation. This project questions how methods of representation determine what and how we see.

When people ask me about the maps I make, I never know what to tell them. Fold it: unfold it. Try to figure out which way is up. Let the map tell you where to go. Try not to use it to get to a place you've been to before. The old map in my car intrigued me, and acquired ever more value for me because it demanded a kind of engagement that most maps do not. The place I wanted to find was never there. It was always just off one edge or another, on a fragment no longer within reach. After a while, the problems with my map became a kind of joke between my friends and me, who also escaped the summer's heat in my car. Over the years, I never bought a new map. Instead, I started going to the places I could find on the pieces that were left.

After I sold my car, I started taking trains. As Reyner Banham has observed, cars are personal motion machines; we steer, stare, and can always stop. Trains, by contrast, are driven by others and afford us time to wonder. They have no glove compartments. Riding the train, I began to look out the window—a lot. Then I started taking pictures. Later, I thought about making maps.

The Nomad Mapping Project is intended as a demonstration of the richness of the urban landscape. Folded like everyday roadmaps, its maps can be read vertically and horizontally, horizontally and vertically. Double-sided, the maps have no front or back, top or bottom, beginning or end. Different panels can be read in relation to one another or separately; each side can be approached as a piece in itself or as part of the "other." Things are discovered and then may disappear under another image or layer of text, only to be revealed at a later moment in a different context, when the folds lay another way. This revealing and concealing suggests the experience of navigating the spaces of the city. Neither can be fully appreciated if traversed along one path alone, or viewed according to only one orientation. They must be approached from many directions, many times over. Reading them, there is always a risk of getting lost.

WINDOW: OVERLOOKING TOMPKINS SQUARE PARK 1990–1995

ANA MARTON

background photo: Winter 1991

DOCUMENTING the city through its gradual adjustments and subtle details, this project is an ongoing process of personal observation and urban representation. Through the window of her apartment building, located on the southern edge of Tompkins Square Park, Marton has been a vigilant witness to the volatility of the park, with its shifting uses and constituencies. In contrast to the *Panorama*'s heroic scope, *Window: Overlooking Tompkins Square Park* explores the city with focused attention. The dedicated observation of this contested space illuminates the metaphor of the mutable city whose forms are often determined by the combined factors of human unrest, social regulation, and natural forces.

In a series of images taken between 1990 and 1995, the project pictures an intimate story of urban transformation. Seen from her window, the fence, sky, trees, and people of Tompkins Square Park form the frame of inquiry. The progressive, time-lapsed images constitute a continuous, cinematic stream of consciousness.   PATRICIA C. PHILLIPS

Summer 1992

"What I see is life looking back at me."

Trinh T. Minh-ha

Fall 1993

"All that is necessary is an empty space of time and letting it act in its magnetic way."

John Cage

Winter 1995

TRANSPARENT CITIES

BRIAN MCGRATH

Video dissolve: Port Authority and interior of Baths.

1. Methodology adapted from Jean-Luc Godard,
"My Approach in Four Movements," in
Godard on Godard, ed. and trans. by Tom
Milne (New York: Da Capo Press, 1972), 239-
242.

Computer models constructed with Mike Lee.
Video prepared by Michael Nagy and Richard
Seaker.

CARTOGRAPHIC LANGUAGE

OBJECTIVE DESCRIPTIONS   **FROM WITHOUT**

MULTIPLICITY: I look at many maps, not one. There are all kinds of cartographic descriptions of the city, from various time periods and sources. When transcribed to the same scale, this material forms an index of mapped elements: natural settings, monuments, historical events, streets, houses, parks, and infrastructure.

URBAN EXPERIENCE

SUBJECTIVE DESCRIPTIONS   **FROM WITHIN**

WANDERING: The space of the city—as experienced, lived in, written about, and filmed—establishes criteria through which the city is re-mapped into fragments and layers: papal, imperial, and national Rome; industrial, colonial, and informational New York.

CINEMATIC LANGUAGE

SEARCH FOR STRUCTURES   **TIME AND MOVEMENT**

MONTAGE: When reproduced as transparencies, the new maps form cinematic cells which can be read individually or in moving relationships. The manipulation of the cells affords simultaneous, non-hierarchical readings: over and under, center and periphery, past and present, seen and unseen, built and demolished. The city is described as a "complex of relationships" rather than as a static object.

TRANSPARENT CITIES

is

AN ATTEMPT TO INFUSE CARTOGRAPHIC LANGUAGE

with

THE LANGUAGE OF CINEMA,

TO MOVE FROM OBJECTIVE DATA TO SUBJECTIVE EXPERIENCE,

FROM WITHOUT TO WITHIN.

LIFE

MIXING IT ALL UP: Meaning in the city does not reside in a privileged location, but is individually created any time, any place. We all construct experiential maps, multiple narratives. Personal stories intercut historical narratives; poetry interrupts planning; the disorder of life displaces the order of the city[1]

ramps and

STREETS

skyscrapers and

farms and

INSTITUTIONS

offices and

TENEMENTS

LANDFILL AND PARKS

marshes and

orchards

PORT AND

transit

STREETS AND

streams

PARKS AND

walls

farms and

zones

subways and highways

WAREHOUSES AND PIERS

ELS AND AVENUES

canals and walls

redoubts and fields

tunnels and air-rights

EXPANSION

INFRASTRUCTURE

GRID   island

MONUMENTS   outpost

fort

farms

subways

zoning

renewal

high-rises

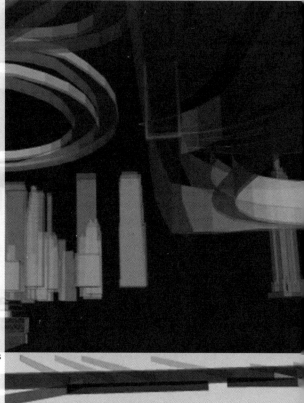

Video still: exploded view from the
Port Authority Bus Terminal towards
midtown towers, with farm lines
below.

NEW YORK

INDUSTRIAL

colonial

informational

PAPAL
national
imperial

MEDIEVAL

CHURCHES   hills

BAROQUE   monuments

VILLAS   roads

      walls

development

institutions

suburbs

infrastructure

CASTLES AND CONVENTS

CHURCHES AND STREETS

      stadiums and roads

      wagons and walls

rail and cars

STREETS AND   hills

ORCHARDS AND   temples

      walls and

ministries

neighborhoods and subways

cars and

PILGRIMS

MARKETS AND VINEYARDS

      river and walls

      baths and

blocks

expansion and

CONTRACTION

      prisons and

CHURCHES

CONVENTS AND   forums

POPES AND   emperors

      emperors and

ministers and

POPES

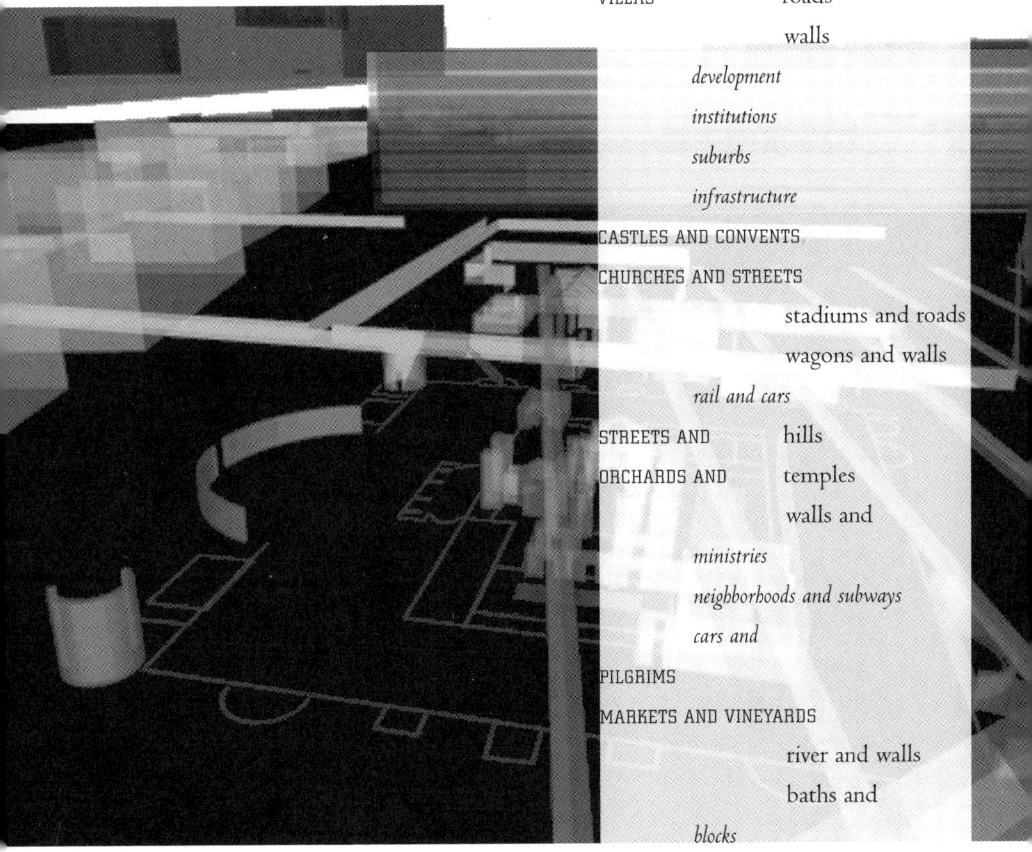

Video still: exploded view from
Termini train platforms towards the
Baths of Diocletian.

ROME

TRANSIT
PLANNING
baroque and christian and medieval and
suburban
CLASSICAL AND
infrastructural and
GATEWAYS AND
EMPIRES AND
ghettos and

WALLS

Video still: exploded view from the
Baths of Diocletian towards Piazza
Republica, with Santa Maria Maggiore
and Termini in the background.

ROME

COMMERCIAL AND
global
information and
headquarters
subways and
farms and
MEDIEVAL
INFORMATION

Video still: view from the New York
Public Library looking west towards
the Port Authority.

NEW YORK

THE HIDDEN CITY

NEWARK METAMETRICS

CITIES as we have known them may no longer be needed. People and industries who have decided they no longer want or need to reside in the urban environment are relocating to rural and suburban areas at an accelerated pace. Those interested in cities are aware of these and other circumstances that call into question the nature and usefulness of the traditional structure and role of our cities. Yet, in Newark—as well as other cities in the New York metropolitan area—there remains a strong sense of identity in the place and its people. For all the strife and distrust, and despite a certain doubtfulness of purpose, Newark is struggling to reestablish itself.

A true consideration of the city entails an examination of this inexplicable sense of identity that binds a people to a place. In this regard, the study

Opposite: *City of Doors: Newark Boys' Chorus*, detail. Photo: Yoland Skeete.
Below: *Roseville Theatre Installation*, view from above. Photo: Paul Warchol.

Newark Metametrics is Thomas Bish, Hal Laessig, and Silvano Sole.

The *Divination Theatre* and the *City of Doors* with *Santa Rosa De Lima* door montage.

of cities is not strictly a study of structure or appearance. Rather, the structure and appearance of the city reflect the shared and evolving mythology of a populace. This mythology is made explicit in the fabricated reality of an embodied political entity: the polis. The necessity of the city, even today, is primarily the need for this common mythology.

In this light, the process of studying a city must be a process of recounting the nature of a mythological entity that is not entirely susceptible to analysis. It requires a selection of approaches and a set of techniques that are as biased and reductive as those of any work of art. A methodology of planning is a fabrication starting with a process of seeing that is inherently political. An example is the *Panorama*, commissioned by Robert Moses: an urban model of miniaturized typological objects ostensibly created for the purposes of ordering and manipulating the city at a grand scale. This subscribes to the conventional mythology that disengages the viewer—and planner—from the unquantifiable sensual experience of the city. We must ask ourselves if the standard tools and

Above: *The Synthesis Wheel.*

Below: *The Divination Theatre,* details of excavated layers.

Baxter Housing Chimney Proposal, detail.

techniques that modern planners have come to use so well—planar and volu-
metric studies, demographics, construction typologies, etc.—are genuine reflec-
tions of the particular urban mythologies that they attempt to address. It may
be that the beliefs in quantifiable structural issues underlying their technique are
obstructions to the experience and shared symbolic associations existing between
the fabric of the city and those who live in it.

Our process of planning distinguishes itself by seeing the artifacts and fabrications of the city as having symbolic values that are sometimes obvious but often hidden. In this regard, a symbol may require one to disregard a virtual reading of the city so that it may reveal a collection of associations. The symbolic references are those that seem to reassert the city as a corporeal entity, a single body with a diversity of parts. The *Synthesis Wheel* and the *Great Map of Newark* present a program for physically and symbolically reconnecting the neighborhoods of Newark. Focusing on the Roseville neighborhood as an example, we have made a presentation of site-specific proposals and contextual materials that will show these symbols as a means of understanding urban diversities: the *City of Doors*, the *City of Song*, the *City of Invention*, the *City of Vocal Anatomy*, and the *City of Religious Experience*.

To understand the city is to recognize a unity that is bound together on many levels. This symbolic city, although dependent on and embedded in the physical city, exists on a different plane. It is a simultaneous city consisting of the connections between its people, institutions, historical events, and places. In considering the representation of such an experience, we have used the idea of a theater as a model for the city as a collective psyche. In developing project proposals emblematic of the Roseville area, we have chosen sites on an associated street in the heart of the city—James Street—in order to make manifest the connections between the center of the city and one of its neighborhoods.

To present these projects for Roseville/James Street, the dioramas and the *City of Doors* set a scene in which the various symbolic elements of the neighborhood and street come into play. In the center, the Divination Theatre uses a selected set of thematic qualities to personify the ideal geography of Roseville within the city limits. The result is an ordering of symbolic sites that one moves past and through, a series of theatrical scenes in which the viewer can begin to assemble various forces at play as seen from the outside and inside.

The revitalization of the city must focus on the re-establishment of a palpable connection between the parts of the city and the city as a whole. For this to be achieved, an embodiment of the interactive connection between the shared human experience of the population and the fabric of the urban environment is required.

SECOND NEW YORK

KYONG PARK WITH WILLIAM CATHCART

Architectural design and text: Kyong Park (Office of Strategic Architecture); computer simulation: William Cathcart (Strategic Design Studio); installation design: Michael Saee; assistants: Micaheal Meredith, Sakoto Hoshino.

AFTER the beginning of the new millennia, cities were no longer centers of economic and cultural activity; families and jobs had forever moved out to the suburbs. Abandoned neighborhoods and buildings came to dominate urban landscapes far more than they had even at the time of "urban renewal." Due to the enormous costs of subsidizing economically and politically alienated populations, some cities were completely bankrupted and abandoned. Others simply turned into suburbs, building shopping malls and tract housing in what had once been city centers. In the end, city governments closed their doors, selling their services and properties to a new ruling class: multi-national corporations.

New York, like other cities, fragmented into a collection of distinct enclaves. Affluent professionals working in the information and financial industries fortified themselves against the homeless, immigrants, and welfare dependents. The city became feudal, comprised of a few wealthy oligarchs and a miserable majority. Governor's Island, protected by hired guards, became a private retreat for the privileged. Central Park was redesigned into a golf club; the Statue of Liberty was converted into a luxury condominium.

The final blow to the city came with the termination of the system of Great Society social programs. Instead, the new national government spoke of "tough love," demanding that welfare recipients take jobs or enter work programs. The right of poor women and children to receive cash assistance was eliminated. Drug and alcohol addictions were no longer considered disabilities. Legal and illegal immigrants were removed from social and welfare programs altogether. There were no jobs for any of these people in the economy, however, and further corporate downsizings left even more people without work. Discontent was widespread and rioting was commonplace. New York burned.

Realizing that assimilation within the prevailing social structure had never been realized—and never would be—the disenfranchised formed a confederation in an effort to end their dependency on the dominant class. Calling for "integration through segregation," this multi-ethnic and inter-class coalition demanded secession from the existing city, and endeavored to build an independent, self-sufficient city of its own.

As all development of the previous society was based on the concept of land ownership, this second society claimed exclusive control of what was free: the air. Resurrecting antiquated air rights legislation, the new society built its habitats right on top of the existing city, bartering the currency of air in order to obtain economic and political means. The skyscrapers of old New York became the pillars of a new, separate city: Second New York.

Various architectural and housing movements developed during the building of Second New York. With Parasitism, a new building was attached to an existing one, stealing energy and material from the host until its evisceration—a reversal of the previous society's exploitation. Recalling the American tradition of "Manifest Destiny," Hybrid-Homesteading saw migratory squatters take possession of unclaimed properties in collective groups. Perhaps the most interesting development was Eco-Logical Architecture, a consequence of the ultimate exhaustion of the earth's natural resources and the subsequent necessity to recycle construction materials. The old city became an open mine where existing buildings were stripped and scavenged to build a new society.

Second New York is a new city built to occupy and destroy the monuments and buildings of a previous authority.

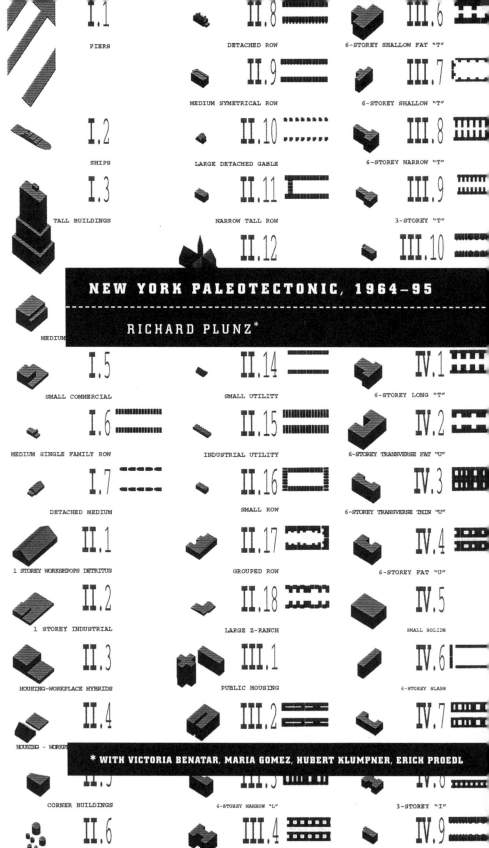

I.1 PIERS

II.8 DETACHED ROW

III.6 6-STOREY SHALLOW FAT "T"

II.9 MEDIUM SYMETRICAL ROW

III.7 6-STOREY SHALLOW "T"

I.2 SHIPS

II.10 LARGE DETACHED GABLE

III.8 6-STOREY NARROW "T"

I.3 TALL BUILDINGS

II.11 NARROW TALL ROW

III.9 3-STOREY "T"

II.12

III.10

MEDIUM

NEW YORK PALEOTECTONIC, 1964–95

RICHARD PLUNZ*

I.5 SMALL COMMERCIAL

II.14 SMALL UTILITY

IV.1 6-STOREY LONG "T"

I.6 MEDIUM SINGLE FAMILY ROW

II.15 INDUSTRIAL UTILITY

IV.2 6-STOREY TRANSVERSE FAT "U"

I.7 DETACHED MEDIUM

II.16 SMALL ROW

IV.3 6-STOREY TRANSVERSE THIN "U"

II.1 1 STOREY WORKSHPOPS DETRITUS

II.17 GROUPED ROW

IV.4 6-STOREY FAT "U"

II.2 1 STOREY INDUSTRIAL

II.18 LARGE Z-RANCH

IV.5 SMALL SOLIDS

II.3 HOUSING-WORKPLACE HYBRIDS

III.1 PUBLIC HOUSING

IV.6 6-STOREY SLABS

II.4 HOUSING - WORKP

III.2

IV.7

* WITH VICTORIA BENATAR, MARIA GOMEZ, HUBERT KLUMPNER, ERICH PROEDL

II.5 CORNER BUILDINGS

III.3 6-STOREY NARROW "L"

IV.8 3-STOREY "I"

II.6

III.4

IV.9

T**HE** final phase of our national "de-urbanization" began in 1964. From that time, the anti-urban policies that originated with the New Deal have been realized in total. In 1937, urbanites comprised 45 percent of our population with only 14 percent living in the suburbs. But by 1990 a suburban majority had been achieved. An emblematic feature of this new post-urban landscape, particularly in New York, is erasure: the loss of workplaces coinciding with the arrival of the economy of consumption in the 1960s; the loss of housing, symbolized by the burning of the Bronx in the 1970s; the loss of hope in the ghettos of the 1980s. Robert Moses was a catalyst for and a true believer in suburbanization. The *Panorama* is more than a histor-

ical monument to his megalomania: its remodeling, which took place from 1988 through 1989, demonstrates the final consequences of his vision of the New York metropolis. The geology of the *Panorama*'s deconstruction indicates just how much was lost. This excavation proceeds chronologically.

LOWER STRATA:

Moving between the major fault lines from left to right.
First the ships stopped coming, their new destinations being the container ports of the urban periphery. Then the piers disappeared, slowly eroding, collapsing, burning. Only a few survive, used for recreation or hauling garbage. Next went the places of production and distribution, many near the piers. On the model, these are the flat "pancake" buildings of all sizes and shapes made of different colors of Plexiglas. With them went the larger of the older apartment buildings. Many were built in the earlier part of the century for members of the working middle class who were enticed to the suburbs after the Second World War, often following their jobs. Most of these apartment buildings were six stories high— a few were higher—and many had elevators. Large investments no longer prof-

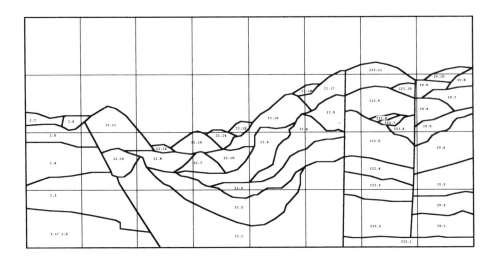

itable for their owners, these buildings could be found in all of the boroughs, the Bronx having the greatest number. In reality, they burned. Such is the nature of the lowest sedimentation. It is the heaviest stuff, consisting of infrastructure, work places, and homes.

MIDDLE STRATA:

Moving along the faults from right to left.

The middle strata represents the next phase of erasure. First, there are the offices and other places of business that were rendered marginal by the decline of industry. Some of these were undoubtedly replaced by the large towers of the post-industrial economy, especially in the midtown area. Much of this debris is surprisingly large, notably that representing the lofts that had disappeared before gentrification led to their conversion from commercial to residential space. Proceeding upward through the layers, the scale of the discarded material moves from large to small. These pieces, the "infill" of the city's neighborhoods, began to accumulate after the marginal industrial sectors fell into decline. Operated by small-building owners, they were the "shophouses"—the small-grain places for production—so essential as support infrastructure for the larger-scale structures; the flotsam and jetsam of the bigger upheaval.

UPPER STRATA:

Upon reaching the upper sediment, the characteristics of the discarded material changes drastically. Here, the detritus becomes progressively more granular; the "sand" of the city of erasure. In this phase of suburban consumption, the vulnerable urban periphery was weakened and, in some cases, cannibalized by clones from beyond the urban border. At this level, the model's materials change from wood to plastic, an ironic correlation of suburbanization with the petrochemical age. The random colors—red, blue, yellow, brown, and white—of these small buildings reflect their apparent insignificance in the eyes of the model's builders. Seemingly negligible, their collective removal will nevertheless have indelible consequences for the city. These buildings would comprise the landscape for future generations, who may forget the foundation of their present. In this we can not take comfort.

Page 68: Chart of detritus types removed from the *Panorama* during renovation. Page 69: *New York Paleotectonic.* Photo: Paul Warchol. Opposite: Sectional map of the strata of detritus coded according to type. Below: Structures taken from the model's surface grouped by type. Clockwise from top left: Six Storey Longitudinal U; Large Detatched Gable; Ships; Six Storey Narrow T.

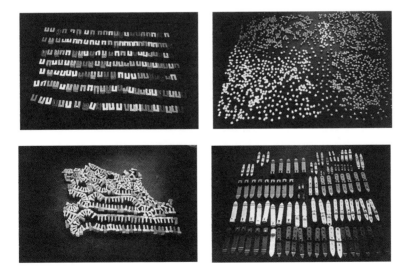

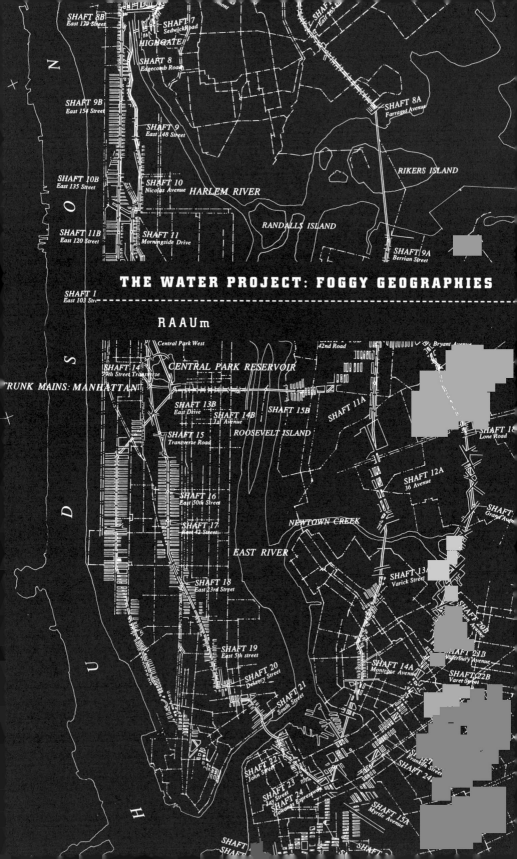

THE WATER PROJECT: FOGGY GEOGRAPHIES

The only works of art America has given are her plumbing and her bridges. MARCEL DUCHAMP, THE BLIND MAN, 1917

WE SUBSCRIBE to the possibly outdated idea that vast public works systems deserve an architectural presence. Further, it is our conviction that social and programmatic innovation is not incompatible with formal invention.

OLD CROTON AQUEDUCT

NEW CROTON AQUEDUCT
GRADE TUNNEL
IN COMPACT AND LOOSE ROCK

NEW CROTON AQUEDUCT
PRESSURE TUNNEL

This project negotiates between the dominant linear character of the water supply system at the local level, and, in contrast, the capillary—or rhizomatic—character of the system as a whole, which includes rivers and streams, topography, watersheds, and complex natural systems. In order to function efficiently, the water supply needs to regulate this wild proliferation. Setting out to discover appropriate strategies, the project makes accessible and visible the complex character of the system at a local level.

New York City is supplied with water by a vast system of reservoirs, aqueducts, and tunnels bored through rock as far as 1,100 feet below ground level. Holding reservoirs and distribution chambers regulate and control the water that is in turn sent into tunnels deep under the city: 110 individual shafts feed up from the tunnels to the 5,733 miles of city water mains. The extent of this nearly invisible system is difficult to comprehend. Water Tunnel No. 3, presently under construction, is the largest public works project in New York, yet the public is generally unaware of its existence.

By calling attention to the vast infrastructure necessary to support the metropolis, architecture can raise the public's awareness of the city as a complex interrelated system. Focusing attention on the system as a whole, new definitions of site are proposed on the basis of a systematic integration of political, regional, and natural factors.

RAAUm is Jesse Reiser, Stan Allen, Polly Apfelbaum, and Nanako Umemoto.

This project was completed with the support of the Graham Foundation.

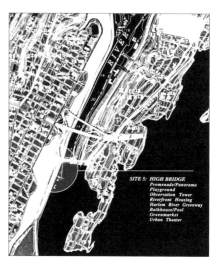

SITE 5: HIGH BRIDGE
Promenade/Panorama
Playground
Observation Tower
Riverfront Housing
Harlem River Greenway
Bathhouse/Pool
Greenmarket
Urban Theater

The Highbridge Development Zone

REGIONAL CROSS SECTION

The site runs the length of the New York City water supply infrastructure: a branching linear system of reservoirs, aqueducts and tunnels stretching from rural upstate New York to the dense network of New York City's water mains. Our definition of site is both unconventionally broad—encompassing over 250 linear miles—yet extremely precise: a vertical and regional cut tied together by a single purpose and administered by the city. By taking the entire water supply system as a site, we utilize a "regional cross section," encompassing the rural areas of the collection reservoirs; the control chambers and holding reservoirs located throughout the small towns and suburban areas of Westchester County; and the distribution sites within New York City.

METHODOLOGY

Consisting of a series of interventions sited along the entire system, this project serves to increase public awareness, to encourage participation through new programs, and to foster new connections between the public and private realms. Design work has progressed through a series of systematically more focused studies. After researching and mapping the entire system, we have concentrated on the right of way of the Old Croton Aqueduct, designated as park land with-

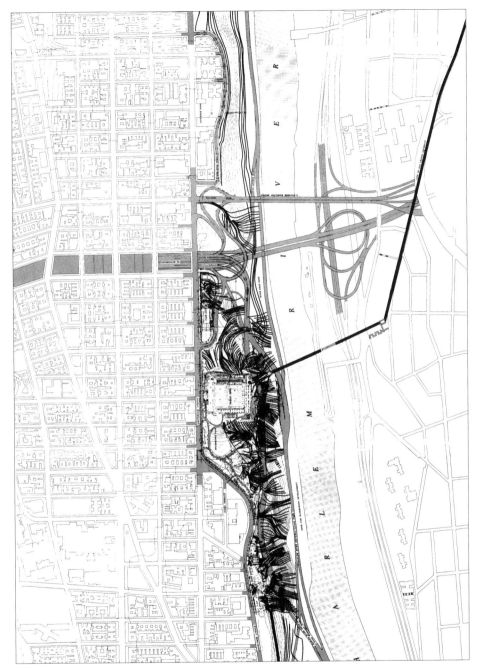

Counter-contour map of Highbridge, Site 5.

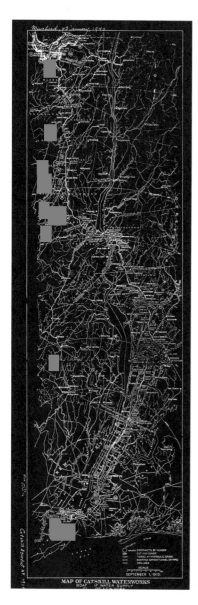

MAP OF CATSKILL WATERWORKS
BOARD OF WATER SUPPLY
OF NEW YORK

in Westchester County. Along this route, we chose three sites that exemplified distinct regional conditions: the Croton Dam in northern Westchester (rural); the Tarrytown interchange (suburban); and the Highbridge in East Harlem (urban).

MAPPING

As a strategy of site analysis, the project proposes a mapping procedure that seeks to uncover shifting site histories and patterns of land use as they are encoded in place names and street designations. French social theorist Michel de Certeau has noted the uncanny persistence of meaning in place names:

> Disposed in constellations that hierarchize and semantically order the surface of the city, operating chronological arrangements and historical justifications, these words slowly lose, like worn coins, the value engraved on them, but their ability to signify outlives its first definitions. . . . A strange toponymy that is detached from actual places and flies high over the city like a foggy geography of "meanings" held in suspension, directing the physical perambulations below.[1]

This "foggy geography" of meaning, a semantic surplus encoded in place names, is selected as a device to generate programs with distinct connections to place while maintaining a detachment that allows for invention and critique.

1. Michel de Certeau, *The Practice of Everyday Life*, (Berkeley: University of California Press, 1984), 104.

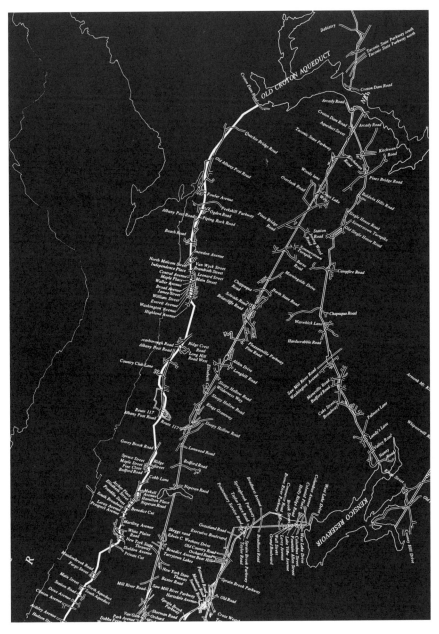

Opposite: Map of Catskill Waterworks.

Above: Water Tunnel, Mid-Westchester.

VISIBLE CITIES

WELLINGTON REITER

MANHATTAN is a vessel, and like all vessels, it is of limited capacity. Inevitably, it has been the fate of the four "outer" boroughs to serve as overflow space. As a result, they are frequently the repositories for that which either can not fit on the island of Manhattan or is deemed undesirable for it.

This process of exportation has spawned a collection of wonderfully idiosyncratic sites, each dedicated to the purpose of housing that which could not remain on Manhattan, from wild animals to giant globes. Not surprisingly, these other "cities" exhibit some of the artifice, density, and encyclopedic variety that characterize Manhattan.

This project calls attention to the satellite cities that orbit Manhattan and allow it to masquerade as a self-sufficient whole. To this end, selected buildings have been exported from the island and fused with reciprocal sites—one from each borough—to form composite entities. The format of these new cities employs a ship-like template borrowed from the metaphor of the vessel to further amplify the nature of these sites as autonomous worlds.

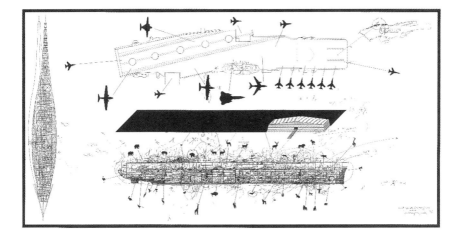

CITY OF ANIMALS AND BIRDS

Technology inevitably becomes obsolete, but ideas too must fade. The eventual retirement of the *USS Intrepid*, an aircraft carrier from the World War II era, was thus a foregone conclusion from the moment it was launched. Proud but inert, the ship now sits awkwardly against the island of Manhattan, avoiding the endangered species list by virtue of its new designation as a museum.

For Noah's Ark, however, a fixture in the old Central Park Children's Zoo, the end came without fanfare. The ark itself was left intact, but the culture that created it had moved on: "There is no place for Noah's Ark in the new Central Park Children's Zoo design, which avoids fairy tales and religious messages," proclaimed an article in the *New York Times*.[1]

These two ships are comparable in other ways. The ark—and the renewal myth of which it is a part—engages the idea of an encapsulated world. In our own time, no vessel has offered such a compelling vision of a floating world as the aircraft carrier, its flat plane being the most haunting of landscapes.

The program of the zoo is both obsolete and yet dedicated to the future. The *City of Animals and Birds* proposes that the two great ships move inland to the Bronx as participants in a mythology that links both past and present, destruction and rebirth. The aircraft carrier will be inhabited by animals and birds. The ark will house the human staff.

1. *New York Times*, September 28, 1995.

CITY OF MAN-MADE OBJECTS

Museums act as filters, removing from circulation those objects deemed important enough to be representative of our highest cultural aspirations. Yet, artifacts entitled to museum protection are insignificant relative to the volume of man-made products that become refuse. These rejected objects, however, also serve as important cultural records. Due to its limited capacity, the island of Manhattan is dependent upon the exportation of its waste, the bulk going to the Fresh Kills landfill on Staten Island. So valuable is this landfill as a historical resource that, like a museum, it also has archivists on site.

Robert Moses, who had transformed the Corona landfill into a World's Fair site, believed that Fresh Kills could also be converted into an amenity for the city: a park and municipal airport. Ironically, Frank Lloyd Wright had imagined a pastoral site for the Solomon R. Guggenheim Museum, and had described its setting in terms that bring to mind the mountainous landfill: "[the museum] would form an individual hill crown, rising up from within and above the new municipal park areas which within a decade will be to Greater New York what Central Park is now to little old New York."[2]

The *City of Man-Made Objects* demonstrates that both the museum and the garbage dump serve as valuable repositories. Its composite image features a conning tower (the Museum of Modern Art, the Guggenheim Museum, and the Whitney Museum of American Art) which surveys an ever-growing landscape of human enterprise.

2 Quoted in R. A. M. Stern, T. Mellins, and D. Fishman *New York 1960* (New York: The Monacelli Press, 1995), 809.

The *City of Man-Made Objects*. Photo: Paul Warchol.

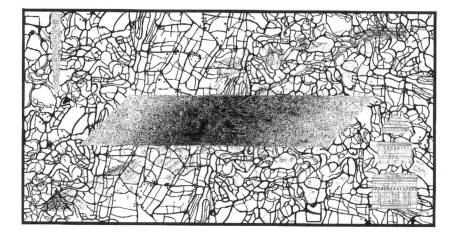

CITY OF MEMORY

For reasons of economics, health, psychology, and space, urban cemeteries have generally been located in areas close to "nature." Could it be that this explains why Manhattan has never felt comfortable with its most significant corpse-in-residence, that of Ulysses S. Grant? His tomb, located on the Upper West Side, is in a sad state of neglect, and there are those who would clearly like to rid the island of its anomalous presence: "We have to remove Grant. [He] has never really belonged in New York," wrote John Tierney in the *New York Times*.[3]

Cleopatra's Needle, moved from the ancient Egyptian city of Alexandria to Central Park, set an extraordinary precedent for the careful and calculated relocation of a monument. The idea of moving monuments, as memory of their origin fades, has been borrowed to create the *City of Memory*.

New York City's most elegant and architecturally rich burial ground is the Greenwood Cemetery in Brooklyn, the "Garden City of the Dead." This cemetery is already the resting place of many Civil War generals, including Major General Henry Wagner Halleck, whom Grant replaced as the head of the Union forces. With the importation of Grant's Tomb into the *City of Memory*, history is allowed to repeat itself.

3 John Tierney, *New York Times*, May 7, 1995.

CITY OF THE WORLD

Robert Moses miraculously converted the Corona dump in Queens into the grounds for the 1939 World's Fair. As if to make clear this feat, he repeated it on the same site for the 1964–65 fair. In fact, the Unisphere—the great symbol of that second fair—is built on the foundation created for the Perisphere, one of the central attractions of the fair of 1939.

In the twenty-five year interval between the two events, Moses sought to make the site the permanent home of the United Nations. His vision of a suburban site for the UN was indirectly supported by Le Corbusier and Lewis Mumford, the latter imagining nothing less "than the building of a complete city," for the organization.[4] In fact, the UN met as a body from 1946–52 in the New York City Building, now home to the Queens Museum of Art and the *Panorama*. Ultimately, the gravitational pull of Manhattan proved too great. The wafer-thin slab of the Secretariat, placed carefully on a pedestal, is a reduction of Mumford's utopian ideal into a digestible unit for Manhattan.

Both world's fairs and even the United Nations are politically artificial constructions representing the idea of shared concerns by the nations of the world. Each has been made redundant by information technologies that link the far reaches of the globe in ways unimaginable in 1939 and 1964. The *City of the World* reunites the UN with its intended site and sets them both adrift.

4 Lewis Mumford, *Progressive Architecture*, August, 1946.

SCORING THE PARK

MARK ROBBINS

ARCHITECTURE embodies a system of order within a given culture and participates in the orchestration of activity. It collaborates to hide or reveal, and serves in this project as a metaphor for the finely crafted system of codings that facilitate the maneuvering of gay men within a network of physical and social settings. The engagement with specific symbols and sites is both derived from necessity and embraced with fastidious and fabulous attention.

This project addresses the area of Central Park known as the Ramble, a space historically associated with a variety of groups including gay men. Here, the Ramble is situated within a dense historical palimpsest of formal and cultural elements that interrelate issues of social control and urban planning. This backdrop includes Frederick Law Olmsted's pragmatic and naturalistic landscape design, the artifice of City Beautiful planning, and the regulating grid of Manhattan.

The City Beautiful movement sought to embellish the industrialized city, ameliorating the lives of its inhabitants without making structural changes

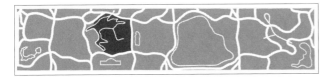

to the society of which they were a part. The appearance of commodiousness was paramount to City Beautiful planners, who provided formal public realms with broad allées and promenades. Olmsted employed this strategy in Central Park, where the main promenade terminates at Bethesda Terrace. His design is both axial and picturesque, with the Ramble "left" as a wilderness of streams, boulders, and gorges. Like the hidden paths of Versailles, it is intentionally off the central axis, signifying a Romantic sense of escape from the constraints of civility, as well as a belief in the curative powers of nature. Called the "soul of the park" it has, since its creation, both served the prescriptions of urban reformers and confounded their plans.

The images of this project are drawn from both archival and contemporary sources and are presented with texts relating to the park's design and history. These include a series of narratives about encounters between men in the park from 1970 to 1990, Olmsted's writings, and accounts of the daily life of the park. This intercutting suggests the complexity of inhabitation both within the park and beyond its boundaries, challenging a simplified reading of historical and modern locales. The intention is to stress the simultaneity of occurrences in this urban setting and the difficult and often ambiguous seam between public and private realms.

At night the park is quiet, remarkable. The moon over its mercury-vapor lamps—of newly-cast art nouveau iron leaves—flattens the color into shades of green, gray, and black. Pools of mist have the luminous glow of a Fantin-Latour. Guys on thin-rimmed bikes pass through in Spandex and sweatbands.

"But the use of a public park—like liberty itself—can be made equitable only by a fair apportionment of the amount of freedoms to be permitted to each class of visitors."

—Frederick Law Olmsted

"Gay men devised a variety of tactics that allowed them to move freely about the city, to appropriate for themselves spaces that were not marked as gay, and to construct a gay city in the midst of, yet invisible to, the dominant city." —George Chauncey, *Gay New York*

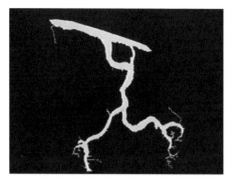

As the artist of New York City's Fresh Kills Landfill, the first task I set myself is to confront the landfill's awesome scale. This has required a parallel attempt to "scale up" my mind, eyes, imagination, and courage while "scaling down" my terror in the face of the landfill. Researching the complex technologies used to map, measure, and monitor the site has provided a means of entry into this daunting place.

Fresh Kills Landfill occupies 3,000 acres on southwestern Staten Island—an area equivalent to three Central Parks—a location chosen by Robert Moses. Nearly a mile long, it will eventually reach a height of thirty-five stories. Fresh Kills is the destination for all of the personal and municipal garbage of New York City. Between 12,000 and 14,000 tons of trash is collected from the five boroughs six days a week, and this waste arrives daily at Fresh Kills in

This project was conceptualized in collaboration with Philip Gleason, Director of Landfill Engineering at the New York City Department of Sanitation. With the support of Sanitation Commissioner John J. Doherty and Deputy Commissioner for Solid Waste and Engineering Martha Hirst, I have been able to realize the beginning stages of a long-term inquiry. I thank the many people who have contributed to this project.

Opposite: Water Creature racing across the landscape. Photo: Mierle Ukeles ©1995.
Above: Aerial photograph of the Fresh Kills Landfill site. Photo: New York City Department
of Sanitation, Landfill Engineering.

twenty barges each carrying 650 tons. The ecologically sound, waterway-based
disposal system employed at the landfill is one of only three similar systems in
use around the world; it is the largest.

The landfill is a space that is inherently in conflict. On the one hand,
it is a symbol of the whole city, a repository, the only city-wide site left to "take
care" of our garbage. Conversely, it is located in a specific locale on Staten
Island. People, animals, and plants live in close proximity to the landfill, and the
largest shopping center in the region sits across the street from it. A marvelous,

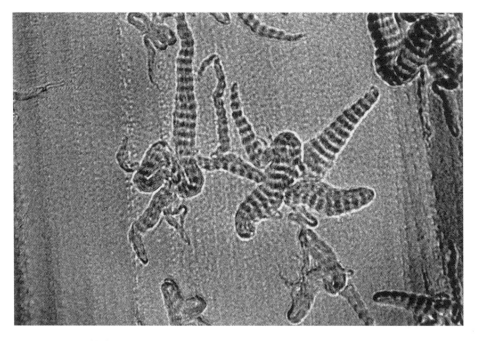

Methanogens, anaerobic single-cell microbes that play a critical role in the decomposition process, the other half of the carbon cycle. Photographed by atomic microscope. Photo: Ray Kass and the Mt. Lake Workshop/Virginia Tech Photo Services.

visible irony persists in the charged zone zigzagging between that place of consumption and the shocking consequences of consumerism.

Over five hundred people work at the landfill, including: bird counters, chemists, crane and compactor operators, engineers, environmental monitors, geologists, landscape architects, metal workers, office administrators, planners, policy analysts, public officials, sanitation workers, soil scientists, surveyors, and restoration ecologists. Along with the Great Wall of China, it is one of only two human-built structures visible from space. Nobody has ever built at such scale with unordered, heterogeneous materials before. Upon completion, it will be the largest human-built structure on the planet.

Noting the landfill's practically unimaginable scale, those who work on site state that it takes years of orientation to learn to find one's bearings there. The comprehensibility and certitude of aerial photos and manipulated

1995

2002

Simulations of the Fresh Kills Landfill in the year 1995 and projected at the estimated time of its closure in the year 2002, as seen from the Staten Island Mall, across Richmond Avenue. Courtesy of New York City Department of Sanitation, Landfill Engineering.

1995

2002

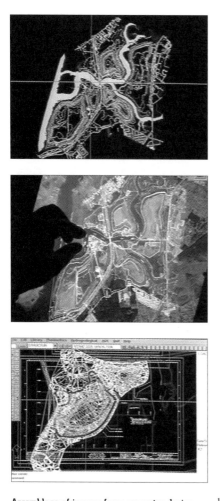

Assemblage of images from computer design programs used for the DM/GIS (Data Management/Geographic Information System) by the Fresh Kills Landfill Engineering Design Team at the New York City Department of Sanitation.

computer-based images vanishes the first moment one steps onto the grounds of the landfill. There is a chasm of difference between advanced systems of representation and the actual experience of observation. Nevertheless, it is impossible to deal with such a complex site without the latest technology. Processing data from the landfill's diverse systems, the Data Management/Geographic Information System (DM/GIS) will bestow a stunning gracefulness when it is fully operational. The DM/GIS assists human decision-making by sorting selected configurations of information into manageable units without smothering policy makers with excess data.

Other high-tech tools assist in the comprehension and planning of the landfill. Ranging from the macro-scale of satellite images to a microscale that reveals anaerobes digesting waste below the surface of the landfill, each imaging system is uniquely fascinating. Sometimes, these systems interrelate coherently; other times, they present contradictory realities. The different forms of representations used on the site include: aerial photos and scanned images; computer imagery; computerbased morphological graphs and quantification graphs; helicopter obliques and aerial photographs; pictures and numbers; pictures and words; video and photographic imagery; and written regulations and depictions of remediation work.

Ideally, these technologies will enable our society to deal with such complex and urgent projects at the highest levels of invention and creativity.

Conversely, technology inevitably raises disturbing questions: imaging methodologies exert influence on our perceptions of the site. How will these systems affect the parameters set to deal with the future of the landfill, its continuing operations, and its progressive closure? Do the integrative capabilities dull us to the profound scale of the waste? What do we envision and overlook? How do visualizations of the landfill influence different experts and lay people? How much do these imaging systems stimulate and liberate or saturate and thus limit our imaginations?

This project attempts to introduce the public to the advanced methods of study and representation used by the New York City Department of Sanitation in the examination and design of the landfill. The Fresh Kills Landfill is the city's most comprehensive, democratic, and social sculpture, a sculpture that we all continue to shape. As such, its many different representations must be understood.

TRACKING NEW YORK'S GHETTOS

CAMILO JOSÉ VERGARA

I have never been able to replicate the sensation of walking through the devastated neighborhoods of the late 1970s and early 1980s, with their newly charred buildings, piles of bricks, and collapsing walls. These scenes were unprecedented in the city. Nobody knew how to explain what was in front of their eyes, yet they recognized that what they saw was of great magnitude. In these apocalyptic places, the separation between my self and my physical surroundings was obliterated. This produced, for hours at a time, the hallucinatory feeling that I could project my consciousness as far as the eye could see, breathe blocks away from my body, and see behind my back.

I help the city tell its own story. Guided by my obsession with the ghetto, I travel to the most destitute neighborhoods. I select the film, camera, lens, light, and angle, and I stare at surfaces soon to be covered by other surfaces and at empty lots waiting for new buildings. I believe that the cumulative character of my photographs and writings makes them a contribution to the annals of the poor.

Above: East New York, Brooklyn, 1978.

East New York, Brooklyn,
in 1980, 1986, and 1994.

The wholesale destruction that afflicted ghetto neighborhoods in New York City during this period could not continue for long. After the razing of thousands of apartment buildings and row houses, the late 1980s saw a surge of construction. The city rehabilitated surviving apartment buildings, and built town houses as well as hundreds of facilities to house the homeless, AIDS patients, drug addicts, and prison inmates.

NORTHEAST EAST NEW YORK ALONG SUTTER AVENUE FROM THE L SUBWAY STATION ON SUTTER AVENUE

For seventeen years, I have kept under observation the two block strips that border Sutter Avenue along the L subway line in Brooklyn. I first visited East New York to see the last remnants of a crumbling neighborhood, once called Little Pittsburgh, where Russians, Poles, and Germans had lived, the birthplace of George Gershwin and Danny Kaye. During the 1970s, the population of this area was reduced to one tenth of its former size, a cataclysmic change. *New York Times* reporter Francis X. Clines compared what was happening to the effect of a virus that attacks the material order of a body. What next, I asked myself? Wanting to find an answer, I periodically returned to the Sutter Avenue stop. The former synagogue, Chevra Sphard of Perry Slaw, is adorned with a sign that reads, "La Sinagoga," but on the roof someone has painted the words "Cristo Viene." The Premier Theatre, the largest structure in the area, was demolished. Atkins Flowers moved next door to the theater, then closed, and then was leveled. Two blocks to the east, a defiant homeowner painted his brick row house green and white, a banner of hope. In the distance, to the east of Sutter Avenue, is Unity Plaza, one of the worst housing projects in the city. The only building to go up since 1988 is a homeless shelter. For a couple of years the empty land of the area was used as a ball field, but it then became vacant again. The few trees growing in the area are behind bars, inside the shelter.

SOCIAL WELFARE AND EXPEDIENT ARCHITECTURE

Methadone clinics are the crudest, most forsaken buildings in New York City, followed closely by mental health clinics and alcoholism units. These structures provide functional space and security, but to the passerby they seem to say, "Go to hell." Addiction is a major force shaping the built environment of poor communities, and these "rehabs" constitute a spontaneous typology that reflects our urban condition.

The use of the synthetic substitute methadone is a common response to heroin dependency. Introduced in 1967, methadone was intended to stabilize addicts, to stop them from committing crimes to satisfy their cravings, and to enable them to function in mainstream society. The drug is less addictive than heroin, with effects that last between twenty-four and thirty-six hours. By contrast, heroin is "effective" for only about six hours.

Outpatient facilities proliferated during the rapid increase of heroin consumption in the early 1970s. In New York State today, about 35,000 people are in methadone programs at a cost of about $4,000 a year per person. Recently, the most powerful argument for the use of methadone has been to slow the spread of AIDS; taken orally, the drug eliminates the risk of infection from contaminated needles.

In an inner-city community, a well-protected building that does not call attention to itself is considered to be an ideal location for a methadone clinic. To house clinics in improvised quarters in medium-sized buildings, the sponsor must block windows, secure the roof, and post guards at entrances. No attempt is made to mitigate the brutal look of these defenses. In the lobby, a clearly visible set of rules of behavior is displayed. Expediency sometimes means that elements of the building's past history—as a theater, bank, supermarket, or garage—can still be seen on the exterior. Sponsors claim that they would love to have a beautiful building, but that they can not afford one.

The exterior changes to the Narco-Freedom building in the South Bronx reflect an uneasy search for an image. Six years ago, this storefront was a dental office. Transformed into a methadone clinic, the roof was given a fence topped with razor wire. In an effort to make the building appear more friendly,

Above: Methadone clinic, Brownsville, Brooklyn, 1988.

Below: Methadone clinic, Crown Heights, Brooklyn, 1990.

the management had murals painted on the facade, one depicting the New York City skyline, the other scenes of Puerto Rico—beaches, palm trees, lovers, and El Morro. When the premises became home to a primary care center—an extension of Narco-Freedom—further measures had to be taken to make the place attractive: two windows were opened up and flower pots were placed on their inside sills; the fence with razor wire on the roof was masked by a green covering; even a tree was planted in front. The organization's chilling name was abbreviated to NF and Community Action Center was tacked on to the end. Now, a private guard on a scooter dissuades people from "hanging out." Narco-Freedom moved its methadone dispensary a few doors down to a windowless storefront.

There is no real need for these outlets. Doctors could simply prescribe methadone to their patients. Clinics, originally planned to provide counseling and housing referrals, now typically offer "no frills" service. Justified only in terms of the benefit they provide to the city as a whole, these shabby facilities are passionately resented at the local level. Neighbors perceive clinics as public nuisances, magnets for troublesome strangers who disturb the peace. With their forbidding exteriors and groups of addicts and former addicts loitering nearby and selling methadone, pills, and other drugs, these outlets are distinguishing marks of poor neighborhoods.

Not having to face the hostility of the neighborhood, day care centers and senior citizen centers announce their names and functions at their entrances. In these structures, only minimal effort is made to achieve a coordinated exterior, and they share the bunker look of the methadone clinics. Yet they appear used and cared for, so that no one would mistake them for being abandoned, and regardless of their stark exteriors, within there is play, socialization, learning, and preventive health care.

Major funding for the exhibition *City Speculations* and the accompanying publication has been provided by:

Office of Queens Borough President Claire Shulman
Natural Heritage Trust/New York State Office of Parks,
   Recreation & Historic Preservation
New York State Council on the Arts